A Farningham Childhood

A FARNINGHAM CHILDHOOD

Chapters from the life of Marianne Farningham

Edited and introduced

by

SHIRLEY BURGOYNE BLACK

Darenth Valley Publications
1988

Darenth Valley Publications
33 Tudor Drive
Otford
Sevenoaks
Kent
TN14 5QP

ISBN 0 9507334 6 6

Printed and bound in Great Britain
by Kingprint International, Richmond, Surrey

This book
is
dedicated
with affection & gratitude
to
Florence Lloyd
and
to the memory of
Alice & Maud Sharwood
great-nieces of Marianne Farningham

Contents

List of Illustrations

Sources and Acknowledgements

The description of Farningham between 1834 and 1855 is based mainly on contemporary parish records filed under the reference P145 at Kent Archives Office (P145/8, Vestry Minutes; P145/12, Poor Rates; P145/5, Church Rates), on parish registers (P145/1), on the 1841 and 1851 census returns for the village, and on items taken from *The Maidstone Journal* over this period. The material on the union workhouse at Dartford was compiled from the Dartford admission registers, also held at Kent Archives Office, reference G/Da.W/a. The details relating to the roads and inns in the village are based on my own work, *Farningham Crossroads: a Study of Two Kentish Turnpike Roads* (1984) and 'Farningham Inns and Innkeepers of the Turnpike Road Era', *North West Kent Family History*, 3/8, 1984.

The chapter on education includes material from Lambeth Palace Library (classes VH2 and VH55), diocesan material held at Canterbury Cathedral Library under G/1.M4, and various references to the parish material listed above, held at Kent Archives Office, where is also the 1819 'Return on Education', under P145/3. This chapter also draws slightly on my own *Children of Farningham and their Schools 1800–1900* (1982).

The chapters on Marianne Farningham's family and on Eynsford Baptist church make use of dissenting records held in the Public Record Office, classes RG4 and RG5, as well as of the minutes of Eynsford Baptist church, 1792–1852, and of the Eynsford Baptist register of births and burials: I am most grateful to the deacons of the Baptist church for allowing me to see these. The Reverend Burnside's notes on his parishioners are held by Kent Archives Office under P145/1.

The principal source for quotations about Marianne Farningham herself, her family and her work is, of course, her autobiography, *A Working Woman's Life*. The Northamptonshire County Record Office holds the Northampton School Board Minute Book 1885–1903 (under ML 1657) and a copy of Marianne Farningham's will (Northants Wills). The County Library in Northampton has a useful collection of ephemera, including a pamphlet issued by College Street Baptist church, Northampton, on the occasion of Marianne Farningham's centenary in 1934, containing reminiscences by two of her friends, M. L. Brice and A. W. Groves. Additional material was obtained from *The Christian World* and *The Sunday School Times*, *passim*, particularly the issues of 18 March 1909 and 26 March 1909 (obituary notices).

I should like to thank Mrs J. Glover, of Eynsford, for her kind permission to quote the two poems from Isabella Rogers' album.

Marianne Farningham's Dr Williams's Library certificate of birth is reproduced by courtesy of the Public Record Office (PRO reference RG5/136). The engraving of Marianne Farningham at the age of 25, and the photograph of her in her 60s are reproduced by courtesy of the British Library; the photograph of her at 50 is reproduced by courtesy of the British Library Newspaper Library, Colindale. The engraving of Eynsford Baptist chapel is reproduced by permission of Kent County Library.

Preface

A Farningham Childhood grew out of an affection for the early chapters of *A Working Woman's Life*, the autobiography of the journalist Marianne Farningham, published in 1907. To say that these first four chapters (here divided into six) have a contribution to make to English history is not to overstate the case. We know from the increasingly sophisticated tabulations of the nineteenth century how many there were of her class: poor, the child of a tradesman, scraping together the rudiments of an education; yet how few of these have left any record of what that life was like. Extremely gifted, Marianne Farningham lived on into the twentieth century, when she wrote, not for posterity, but for 'a few friends', an account of her early years in the Kentish village 19 miles from London where she grew up.

In many ways a story of hardship and privation, it is one that is softened by the beauty of the surrounding countryside, to which she was sensitive from a very young age, and by her own sunny optimism, a characteristic which was to come more to the fore in later years. Her life was an almost exact mirror of the Victorian era – she was born three years before Victoria came to the throne, and died eight years after that reign came to an end – and not less representative of it for her being a devoted member of a nonconformist church; this account of her youth could accurately have been called 'A Victorian Childhood'. But that would have been to give it a title already loaded with assumptions, which would in no way have prepared the reader for the life of a little girl that consisted of 'much running about in the open air', and who did not own a dress with long sleeves until she joined the church at the age of fourteen. For this reason, I have preferred a title more intimately connected with Marianne Farningham herself, and which she can fill with the events of her own life, unhampered by the hardening preconceptions of a later age.

The Introduction is intended to provide a more detailed setting of the village of Farningham in the first half of the nineteenth century than could have been known to a child, as well as to fill out the story of Marianne Farningham's later years and of her success as a journalist.

April 1988   Shirley Burgoyne Black

PART I

Introduction

1

The Village of Farningham, 1834–1855

I

In many respects 1834, the year of Marianne Farningham's birth, marked a turning-point between the old ways and the new. 1834 was the year of the 'martyrdom' of the six agricultural labourers from Tolpuddle, in Dorset, who were transported for seven years for their part in the administration of a trade union oath, the year in which the passing of the Poor Law Amendment Act, by grouping parishes into unions with a single workhouse, threatened to destroy the individual life of the villages, the year in which a rapid succession of Prime Ministers (Grey, Melbourne and Peel) showed the volatility of the times, the year in which the old House of Commons itself was destroyed by fire, symbolically as it were adding itself to a blaze of old wooden court of exchequer tallies. It also happened to be the year in which a young and somewhat giddy princess of fifteen passed three months in Kent with her mother, staying in the fashionable spa town of Tunbridge Wells, and spending a night, before going on to Hastings, at the Sussex Hotel (later to be renamed the Royal Victoria and Sussex) where 'in the evening, the front of the Hotel was tastefully illuminated, Chinese lanterns being suspended in the trees'.

The decade of the thirties was to prove one of wholesale innovation, of a sweeping away of what were seen as the old, bad, ad hoc ways, and an attempt to replace them positively with complete new systems, which it was intended should be more efficient, more in keeping with the Britain of the nineteenth century and also – bearing in mind how indebted those who framed the new systems were to the thinking of the Benthamites and the Utilitarians – more productive of the general good. Thus Parliament itself had been reformed in 1832, extensive municipal reforms were to be carried out in 1835, the Registrar General's office was legislated for in 1836, establishing local registries in districts based on the Poor Law unions, while in the same year the vexed system of church tithes was finally abolished with the Tithe Commutation Act. The practice of slavery, made illegal in England and Wales in 1807, was finally outlawed in 1833 in the West Indian colonies where it had been practised on a large scale, thus paving the way for reforms in Britain, particularly with regard to the treatment of women and children in mines and factories. And this legislation does not reflect the growing proliferation of railway lines all over the country, nor the numerous committees set up to investigate such matters as public sanitation in towns and education for the masses, nor the inauguration of a new, and, as it was to prove, important reign in 1837.

The Farningham of Mary Ann Hearn was only slowly affected by these changes and indeed, as a small, quite well organised village community, had far less need of them than the great industrial centres. She herself says, 'I had the good fortune to be born in the country', and one only has to turn the pages of Edwin Chadwick's *Sanitary Condition of the Labouring Population of Great Britain*, the report of one of the committees mentioned above, which came out in 1842, with its horrifying revelations of courts and basements awash with human excrement and of burial grounds oozing the products of human decomposition, to realise that in many respects a small community set in the countryside had considerable advantages over a town.

Not every village was a participant in events which acquired national proportions during this period. Chartism, for example, does not seem to have touched Farningham or to have made very much headway in Kent generally. Landlords and farmers had been sufficiently shaken by the Swing riots of 1830, which had been particularly violent in Kent, to make conciliatory gestures towards their labourers and were mindful throughout the 1830s and 40s of what we would now call industrial relations: many of the local agricultural associations, which seem eventually to have covered the whole of Kent, were set up in the early 1830s: the Kentish Agricultural Association (later the West Kent Association) appears to have been founded in 1833, the Holmesdale Association in 1831. We still find them thriving in the 1850s, rewarding ploughmen and their drivers, shepherds, labourers who had raised the largest families without asking for relief, servants who had worked for the same master for the greatest number of years. During the Chartist era, on the contrary, the county had its own positive rallying cry, that of Protection, which fought first the threat, and later, until well into the 50s, the fact, of the 1846 repeal of the Corn Laws. Repeal struck at the heart of an agricultural, corn-growing county such as Kent. It was firmly opposed by almost all the county MPs over this period, two of whom, Sir Edmund Filmer and William Masters Smith, were frequent and welcome visitors to Farningham. The Anti-Corn Law Leaguers, where they existed in Kent, would seem to have belonged largely to an informed middle class, inhabitants of towns rather than of villages.

II

The autobiography of Marianne Farningham, born Mary Ann Hearn on 17 December 1834, is, like all autobiographies, a very personal story. She does not set out to give us the history of her village, but rather that of the little girl who grew up there. Nevertheless, in the pages of *A Working Woman's Life* we glimpse something of the densely patterned background against which her early life took place; the terraced Hearn cottage was not the only one which must at times have been full to overflowing with people: in 1821 there had been 97 houses for the 137 families in the village and even in 1831 the ratio was still 121 to 130. Geographically, Farningham was somewhat bigger then than it is now, extending in the north-west considerably further along the London Road into what is now the separate parish of Swanley, and including Button Street and Mountain (now Moultain) Hill. Curiously, however, its population figure was wholly stable throughout Mary Ann's childhood: the census figure for 1831, 1841 and 1851 is an unvarying 701, and although this clearly masks the arrival of newcomers and the departure of many of the village's youth and others in search of the employment that Farningham could not provide, the atmosphere within this small Kentish village remained in many ways very largely unchanged over the whole period 1834 to 1855.

1834, indeed, found the parish of Farningham very much as it had been thirty or even forty years earlier. The almost doubling of its population over this time (in 1801 it had been 397) had made very little difference to the structure of the village. A parish which had been divided among a number of landowners for many years (several of them resident elsewhere), Farningham remained in the 1830s, as in the 1790s, in the hands of around 30 owners. Its manor had been virtually defunct for some time, although the village had a nominal squire throughout the nineteenth century: Thomas Fuller, father and son, until 1822, and then Thomas Waring (who inherited through his wife Sarah, daughter of John Fuller) and his son William. The same parish officers were guiding and controlling the affairs of the parish as they had done for centuries – vicar, curate, churchwardens and parish clerk, constable, highway surveyors, overseer of the poor and assistant overseer.

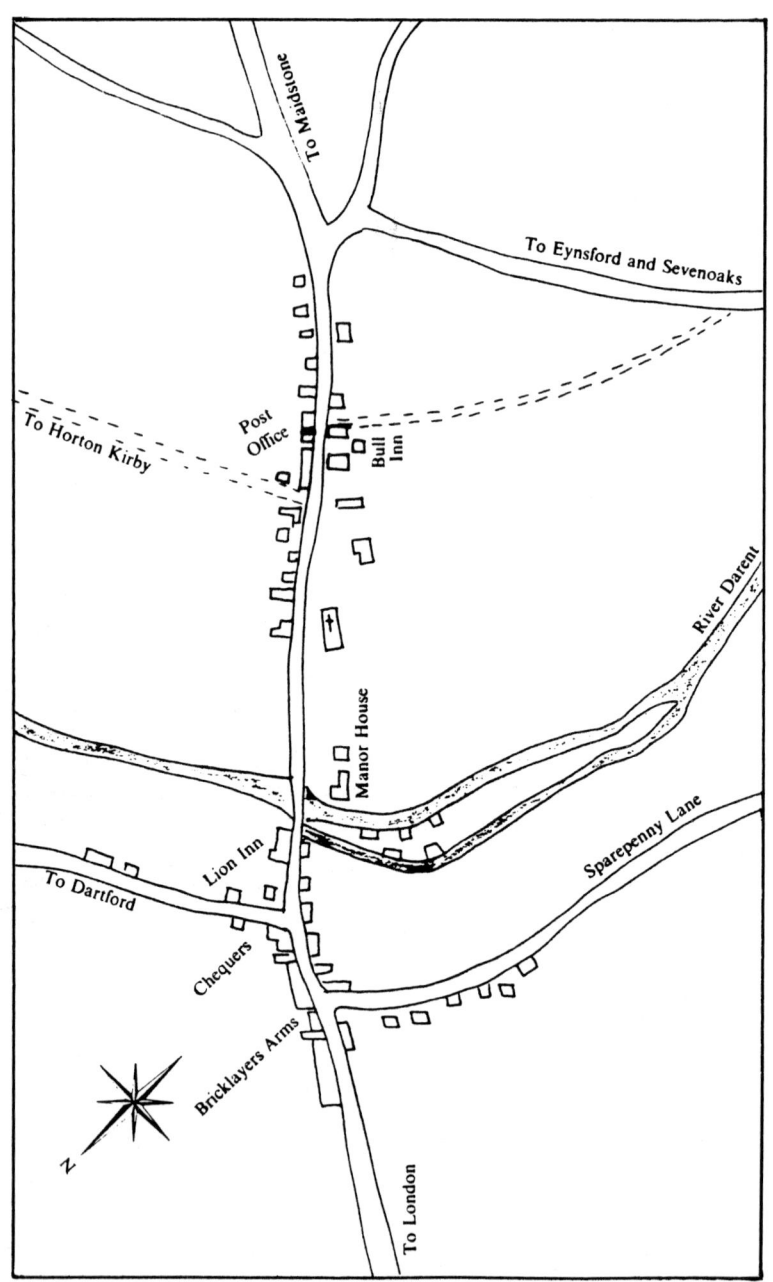

Plan of the village of Farningham around 1840.

Based on the map prepared for the commutation of tithes in Farningham and on an 1828 map of the London turnpike road through the village.

Until 1836 the village was still running its own poorhouse and thus generating from the poor rates its own micro-economy. This took the form of payment for the mistress of the poorhouse and for the seemingly short commons which were doled out by her to the inmates, as well as for its furnishings and fittings – 'basons' and plates, sheets, blankets and bolster cases, mops and brushes, tubs and pails, bavins* for the fire, clothes for its living and coffins for its dead – and for the necessary services: cutting hair and specking* boots, tending the sick and sitting up with the dying. The parish was still concerned with finding apprenticeships for some of its boys until well into the 1850s (Marianne Farningham's future brother-in-law, Thomas Sharwood, was apprenticed to George Ayliffe, a tailor, for 6 years in 1848), and by and large there were the same occupations to be found in 1834 as there had been in 1794 in this village, which, with one important qualification, was one of the many agricultural villages in Kent.

The majority of Farningham's seven hundred people lived along the bare half-mile that constituted the principal part of the village, between the Bull and the Bricklayers Arms, sometimes known simply as 'the street'. While many of these were agricultural labourers, who tramped out to work each day on one of the village's six principal farms (the Manor or White Hill Farm – earlier known as George Farm – Chimham's, Charton, Pedham Place, Beesfield and Eglantine), a number of them exercised their callings within the village. Here were to be found the butcher Francis Martin, the two bakers Henry Gregory and Thomas Turner, the grocer and draper William Atwood, and the milkman Charles Stanford, as well as the tailors George and Rickeby Wallis, two of the village's four shoemakers, Thomas Wood, and Marianne Farningham's own father, Joseph Hearn, the hairdresser Stephen Pope, the watchmaker Jacob Hankins, the cabinet-maker George Le Feuillade, and the painters and glaziers, Martha Stockley and her son John. It was here that the sounds of their work would have led you to the wheelwright James Petman, the three village blacksmiths, William Gibson, Henry Mandy and Robert Hales, the saddler John Gandy, the carrier and the carter, Thomas Dray and Henry Heath, the mason Joseph Woolley and the stock castrator Francis Booker, while here too – perhaps also characterised by sound – lived the vicar, the schoolmaster and the surgeon, in the persons of the Reverend Benjamin Sandford (otherwise Winston, more usually represented by his curate, the indefatigable Reverend Andrew Burnside), Charles Everest, and Dr Frederick Hunt. And in the heart of Farningham, just across the road from the Lion, the large and elegant

---

* Bavins, specking: Kentish dialect words. Bavins: brushwood faggots for kindling. Specking: fitting iron tips to the toes and heels of boots.

corn-mill on the Darent, belonging to the Colyer family, provided ample work for a miller and several journeymen.

This list of some of the inhabitants of Farningham in 1841 was not of course exactly replicated in 1851. Nevertheless there was in the village over the period 1834 to 1855 what one might call a remarkable permanence of personalities, from the vicar down. It is true that the Reverend Benjamin Sandford resigned the benefice in 1848 in favour of his curate, the Reverend Andrew Burnside. But Mr Burnside, appointed to the curacy in 1821, had been the principal minister in the parish since 1832, when Sandford obtained his first licence for non-residence on account of ill-health, and he was to remain in the parish until his death in 1863 at the age of 69. (Sandford did not die until three years later, in Rhyl, North Wales, when his body was brought back to Farningham for interment.) James Sharp, parish clerk to both these gentlemen, had been appointed in 1811 in the time of William Van Mildert, and he lived to the age of 84, dying only in 1871. He is very likely the 'Mr Sharp' of Marianne Farningham's story. The doctor, who makes more than one appearance in her autobiography, is probably on each occasion Dr Frederick Bell Hunt, who had been present at her birth, who provided a report on the health of the district which is referred to in Carleton Tufnell's pamphlet of 1841, *On the Dwellings and General Economy of the Labouring Classes in Kent and Sussex*, and who died in 1859, aged 53. The philoprogenitive village school-master Charles Everest (who appears to have had 19 children, by his two wives Margaret and Annette) was another familiar figure during this time. Assistant overseer for many years, wheelwright and even inventor, he survived until 1857.

Throughout this period most of the land in the centre of the village belonged to the Colyers and the Warings, and in spite of the number of people it accommodated it was still remarkably open, with the villagers' houses and cottages concentrated at each end of 'the street' and at the openings of a few lanes and roads off it. Along the southern side of the road lay the most prestigious buildings: the parish church of St Peter and St Paul surrounded by its churchyard, the manor house, the vicarage and the mill, all with considerable grounds, as well as several large gardens and a rookery. On the northern side lay Mr Waring's paddock – the meadow beyond it being perhaps the earlier much loved George Meadow, and one or possibly both of these used occasionally for market and fair – the grounds belonging to the Lion inn, and some fair-sized gardens, including Miss Colyer's and Mr Rogers'. Within this half-mile there were in fact four village inns, three of them with land attached which was used principally for the grazing of horses, an important element in the economy of the village. The two oldest, the Bull and the Lion, lay one on each side of the Darent – the Lion, indeed, with its grounds sloping right down to the river and possibly facing, originally, straight across the former 'ancient bridge' which had been replaced in 1773 by the present one slightly to the south of it. The Bull was the only inn on the southern side of the street: the Chequers and the Bricklayers Arms, which came somewhat later, both stood on the northern side of the road through the village which, as part of the London to Maidstone road, was turnpiked in 1752.

It was the turnpiking of its main road, combined with the village's position on it, which had made of Farningham something more than just another agricultural parish. Foots Cray, with its inn the Tiger's Head, and Kings-down, with its Game Cock, lay along the same road to west and to east, but there is no indication that they ever attained the standing of Farningham, positioned as it was almost exactly halfway along the 36 miles between London and Maidstone. In the days of slower travel, that is to say, up to about the end of the eighteenth century, Farningham had provided a very good place to put up for the night, and its two principal inns throve accordingly, the Lion in particular being favoured with the patronage of the gentlemen of the county – lords, ladies, land-owners, members of parliament and justices of the peace – while the stage-coach trade went to the Bull. Additional importance was given to Farningham by the fact that a minor turnpike road crossed the London road here. The Dartford–Sevenoaks road, although of course by no means as busy as the London–Maidstone road, was nevertheless a successful turnpiking which lasted from 1766 until 1865. Almost mid-way between Dartford and Sevenoaks, Farningham again found itself conveniently located, and for many years the trustees of the lesser road held their meetings and auctioned their tolls at the Lion inn. The turnpiking of these two roads brought considerable prosperity to Farningham, both directly and indirectly, and raised it to a position of importance from which it did not fall until after 1860. A direct consequence of the business brought by the roads was the opening of three more inns to cater for passing traffic: the Chequers (usually termed a public house, rather than an inn) which stands on the corner of the Dartford Road, came into being towards the end of the eighteenth century; the Bricklayers Arms, opposite the end of Sparepenny Lane, was built around 1805, while further out of the village, on Mountain Hill, the Hop Pole was opened in 1828, soon adding a race-course and pigeon-shooting to its attractions, to tempt the officers down from Woolwich.

The inns must have been the source of constant noise by day, and sometimes at night, too. In 1839, for example, no fewer than six Maidstone coaches were passing twice a day through Farningham, calling at the Bull on their way up to London and back again: the British Queen, the Reliance, the Balloon, the Tally-Ho!, the Times and the Favorite. These were joined on a Monday, Wednesday and Friday by Martin's Omnibus, also from Maidstone, while other villages along the way probably contributed their own less sophisticated and slower conveyances, vans and carts. For some years William Hollands was running a coach daily from Farningham itself up to London and back, in the summer months at least, and when he turned to inn-keeping in the 1840s, E. Luther, of West Malling, took the coach over and continued it as a London coach. Luther seems to have called at the Lion inn, but the majority of the stage coaches called at the Bull, just opposite the Hearn cottage, and the dusting which Mary Ann was called on to do by her mother was by no means an invention designed to keep her out of mischief, but something which needed doing, and needed doing frequently, as each coach, drawn by its four horses, clattered into the courtyard of the Bull from the stony, unasphalted road.

The heavy use which was made of these roads, and the frequency with which coaches and carriages – barouches and landaus, clarences, stanhopes and britzskas, domestics and phaetons – stopped in the village, were thus the source of additional types of employment, such as waiter, hostler and post-boy, over and above those of agriculture; a local comment on the 1821 census figure for Farningham, for example, notes the influx of horse-keepers into the village. The 1841 census names six of them, some, like John Norris and William Russell of the Bull, obviously attached to an inn, others, like Jesse Brenchley and George Bevis, perhaps self-employed.

This was already a period of lamentations in many places as railways began to compete with roads, inevitably stealing custom and traffic from them – albeit in a piecemeal fashion. Railway time bills of the late 1840s give the rates for carrying horses and two- and four-wheeled carriages as well as passengers, showing that railways were initially regarded as purely complementary to the roads – a journey to the railway station, perhaps at a considerable distance from one's residence, being made in one's own carriage, which after being carried on the railway would be brought into use again for the final lap of the journey. But such a cumbersome mode of travelling could not remain in favour for long, and trains were eventually being met by omnibuses from all the local villages and towns. In 1857 the Reverend Jonathan Whittemore, coming home after a week spent in London at his publishing business, is on the omnibus bringing him from Dartford station to Farningham when he passes Marianne Farningham and her friends walking to Foots Cray. By the mid-1850s a train journey up to London from Dartford (whose station on the South Eastern Railway's North Kent line had opened in 1849) was clearly chosen by many local travellers in preference to a stage-coach journey by road. Nevertheless, Farningham, which was perhaps initially inimical to the notion of the railways, seems to have been successful in retaining a considerable amount of its road traffic throughout the time that Mary Ann Hearn was a girl there.

III

In Farningham the first major casualty of the Poor Law Reform Act, which was not brought into effect locally until 1836, was the village poorhouse, although this was later continued as the Roper Charity House and as such provided as before a kind of alms-house accommodation for the elderly poor of the parish. The vestry meeting, which had formerly controlled its destiny and with it that of its inmates, no longer had the power of deciding when the boys of the poorhouse should have their shoes 'tipp'd and heel'd', or what should be the weekly allowance to the parish's needy — which always included a string of girls with illegitimate babies. One of the last beneficiaries from the 'old' system of parish relief, which was discontinued with the implementation of the Poor Law Reform Act, was Thomas Taylor, who received in May, 1836, 'a new Round Frock and two pair of Stockings and a new Hat'. It now became the duty of the overseers, a duty performed almost invariably by the assistant overseer, Charles Everest, to give those who qualified for relief an order to go into the union workhouse at Dartford.

   We do not in fact find many Farningham people entering Dartford workhouse in its early years. Initially it seems to have been used to tidy the villages of their stray orphans and elderly sick: in the summer of 1837 there was a big transfer of children from Bexley (used for the reception of children before the large mixed workhouse at Dartford was built) to Dartford, ten of them being originally from Farningham: James, Jane, George and Matilda Meopham; William, Sarah and Charles Jordan; Richard Boakes; John Barton; George Allen. On later occasions when single children are admitted they are frequently 'rescued' after a short time, sometimes even by the relative who has been said to have deserted them. George Packman, aged 12, who was admitted in 1838 and described as 'deserted by mother', was discharged the same year at the request of his father. From his later history, however, he seems to have been a difficult boy who would perhaps today have been taken into care, and there is no doubt that the new institutions, with their greater facilities, were able to cater for problem families, thus highlighting many things which an earlier age may have preferred to ignore.

Farningham offers the example of at least one such family over this period, as poor Sophia Simmons and her children drift in and out of the workhouse like slow-moving yo-yos. Sophia, aged 23 and described as a servant who has been deserted by her husband, is first admitted in November 1836, with Elizabeth aged 1 and Eliza who is only a month old. She was discharged in December, but re-admitted in January, as before, only to be discharged in April at the request of the formerly deserting husband. By the end of 1849 she had been admitted and discharged several times, usually at her husband's request, and three more children had been born to her, Thomas and George definitely, and Jane probably, 'in the house'. The husband, Thomas, having in the meantime served a three-month prison sentence at Maidstone, was now in the workhouse with them. Unsuccessful attempts were made by the authorities to place Eliza, and perhaps Elizabeth also, in service, and in 1850 the whole family was discharged – to what conditions, particularly for Sophia, one can only surmise. Overall, however, the workhouse seems to have been functioning more and more as an infirmary, to which the elderly sick and ailing, and the young in the event of an accident, were consigned for a period which seems always to have been as short as possible, since inmates were frequently 'Discharged at own request' after only a few days.

The mixture of concern and helplessness felt by the parish vestry in the face of cases with which it was no longer called upon to deal is perhaps typified by that of David Dalley and his wife, which arose in 1844. Dalley, a labourer, was in regular employment at Chimham's Farm, where he earned ten shillings a week, but he claimed that he was unable to find either home or lodging in Farningham or in any of the neighbouring villages. Perhaps Dalley himself slept at the farm, but it was with the wife that the parish's letter of February 1844 was concerned, spelling out the whole misery of her condition:

> Meantime, the woman who is a miserable object, and liable to frequent and severe Epileptic fits, is, with her three children, obliged to get at night what shelter she can in sheds and farm buildings. During the day, she is frequently wandering about the village — and has repeatedly fallen into fits in the street and churchyard, under the influence of which she has more than once been seen with her person perfectly exposed.

The letter continues:

> The Vestry feel, that though they are desirous that something should be done – they have no *power* to act. They are aware, too, that under common circumstances the Board declines granting any relief – the Husband being in regular work.

The suggestion is made that the Board might consent to Mrs Dalley being admitted into the Union house if the husband were forced to pay something towards her support, and the letter concludes:

The Vestry consider that in thus laying the case before the Board of Guardians they exonerate themselves and the Parish Officers from any blame, if, in consequence of one of these fits, Mrs Dalley without home or shelter, should some day be found dead in the Public Road.

There is ample evidence that the giving of outdoor relief – that is, relief to applicants who did not enter the workhouse – was fairly soon resumed, but this seems to have been done from the workhouse itself and did not involve parish authorities as such. Obliged to turn its attention to things rather than people, the vestry discussed with some heat the provision of church fires from church rates, ordered the repaving of the footpaths through the village from the Bricklayers Arms to the post-office with Kentish rag curbstone, and the lowering of the causeway (it must have been earlier at least a foot above the road) to six inches, reported cases of nuisances to the Board of Guardians, and requested tenders from local wheelwrights for the repair of the churchyard fence. With the removal from it of responsibility for people, however, its life-blood had begun to drain away, and from 1852 onwards one occasionally comes across the despondent entry 'Nothing done' in the vestry minutes.

IV

There can be little doubt that the emasculation of the parish vestry coincided with a decline in village life, due partly to the repeated failure of harvests and the hard times experienced all over England and Wales, as well as in Ireland. We find several mentions of benevolent charity in Farningham over this time, mainly taking the form of the provision of bread and fuel. In March 1842 a correspondent to *The Maidstone Journal* (quite possibly Mr Burnside, the curate) noted that,

Many philanthropic persons both individually and conjointly have, in a manner highly creditable to themselves, endeavoured to mitigate the hard conditions of the poor in this village by bestowing a part of their abundance towards alleviating their distresses. A lady, distinguished for her benevolence, has given bread weekly to the amount of three hundred loaves. Coals also have been purchased by subscription, and have been delivered weekly at the rate of 6d per bushel, the money collected being added to the stock.

Charities of this kind were a regular and, for many, a humbling experience of life during this decade, not only in the villages: for some years Maidstone ran a Bread Charity for which tenders were requested. Well into the 1850s, severe weather could bring hundreds of applicants to the workhouse, begging for relief, as in February 1855 at Dartford, when,

> The guardians, being desirous to meet the immediate wants of the poor, ordered that each applicant should be relieved, and the contractor could not meet the unusually large demand until a late hour on Sunday afternoon

– whether for bread or coals, we are not told. Around the same time, *The Maidstone Journal* continued,

> a numerous body of men paraded the streets of the town, calling at every house and presenting a petition soliciting relief, which was very liberally afforded by the inhabitants generally, and matters all went off very quietly.

Marianne Farningham's youth was undoubtedly passed closer to those who did not always have enough to eat than to those who could afford to dine at the Lion. For her, the mid-fifties were the years in which

> it was borne in upon me that I must leave home, and go away to earn my own living, for my father's life was a struggle, and it was difficult to make both ends meet.

Here, indeed, was something which had changed little within the village from 1834 to 1855. However, those not encumbered with the need to find a dependable daily wage were free to develop the ideas with which the period was fermenting, and, with them, Farningham entered the fifties on the crest of the wave of optimism which characterised this high-Victorian period. This is apparent in three key areas, agriculture, machinery and railways, in all of which there were exciting developments at the beginning of the decade.

In 1851 a monthly stock market was begun in Farningham and appears to have continued for a number of years. At the beginning of 1852, partly, it would seem, as a result of a disagreement with the millers of Dartford, a weekly corn market was also started, and held in a room at the Lion inn. The annual fair was still a feature of the village on the 15th October, although here the emphasis seems to have been slowly turning from cattle to horses. In addition, the West Kent Exhibition of Poultry, Pigeons and Rabbits was begun in 1853. Not only this, but in the same year the local agricultural association shook itself free of aristocratic patronage, which seems too seldom to have materialised into an aristocratic presence for the liking of its members. After considerable debate and soul-searching, the West Kent Agricultural Association was reconstituted by local farmers themselves as the Dartford and Farningham Agricultural Association. By 1854 this had become the Darenth Vale Agricultural Association, regularly holding an autumn plough-ing match, often in a field belonging to a Farningham member.

Closely connected with all these moves was William Dray, a Farningham-born man and a farmer, whose principal interest at this time was the manufacture of a variety of agricultural implements under licence: we find them advertised regularly in the local press. Dray had a warehouse at Swan Lane, London Bridge, but frequently showed his machinery in operation on his farm. He also attended a number of exhibitions up and down the country with it, where he appears to have been highly successful. In the early 1850s, as well as promoting a reaping machine locally, he was clearly a great influence in converting local farmers from the old Kent plough, the turn-rise, to the more modern iron plough. He appears to have been an energetic and likeable man and a prominent member of the committee of management of all local agricultural undertakings.

Dray seems also to have been one of the prime movers behind the Darenth Valley railway, planned initially to run from Dartford to Farningham, and incorporated by special Act of Parliament in the session of 1853, by which time local opposition to a railway seems to have been stilled. This short line, which would have connected with the North Kent at Dartford, was intended to make of Farningham a 'local rendezvous' for Sevenoaks, Wrotham, Ightham, Kemsing, Otford, Shoreham, Eynsford, Swanley, Chevening, Chipstead, Riverhead and Sundridge, with stations at Dartford, Hawley, Darenth, South Darenth and Horton Kirby as well as Farningham itself. There is no doubt that this branch line was quick off the mark. By the end of 1853 no fewer than six other local lines were notifying to the public their intention to apply to Parliament for authorisation: the London and West Kent; the West Kent and Crystal Palace Junction; the Sydenham, Farn-borough and Otford; the Southwark and Crystal Palace; the Otford, Sevenoaks and Tonbridge; and the Maidstone and Ashford Junction. At this stage the future must have looked bright indeed to the promoters of the Darenth Valley Railway, already in possession of their Act of Parliament, but the hopes of their small scheme were to be extinguished by larger projects, and it had eventually to be abandoned.

V

While the traditional occupations of agriculture, the dissemination of the new machinery and the phantasma of a local railway were being pursued in deadly earnest, they sometimes burgeoned into what was one of the lighter episodes of nineteenth century life. This took the form of a public dinner, usually held at the Lion inn, where mine host, by now James Painter Davis, received regular accolades for his 'indefatigable catering'. At the end of the dinner, when the cloth had been removed, it was not unusual for a stream of toasts to be drunk, ranging from 'the Queen' to 'the Press', who often reported such occasions at length. The dinner which followed one of the early corn markets, in February 1852, was a particularly splendid occasion, with an appropriate song following every toast. Thus 'the Queen' was followed by the song 'England's Victoria', and 'Success to Farningham Corn Market' by 'I'm for freedom of opinion' – a reference to the dispute which had led to the setting up of this somewhat schismatic corn market in the first place. The health of the chairman, Sir Percival Hart Dyke, who had supplied venison for the table from his park at Lullingstone, was graced by the song 'Thirty Years Ago' while 'Lady Dyke and the Ladies', a toast drunk very much *in absentia*, was followed by 'England, Europe's Glory', and the much-loved Mr James Russell of Horton Kirby was hymned with 'The Old English Gentleman'. The principal singer, Mr Thomason, who appears to have been a Londoner and a colleague of William Dray, was himself the subject of a toast towards the end of the proceedings.

Music was an indispensable part of the life of this, as of numerous other local villages, where ringing days still, as in the eighteenth century, provided a long carillon several times a year. No show or feast day was complete without its music, and while small events, such as the anniversary of a friendly or benefit society, relied for their processional accompaniment on village talent, larger ones imported it from outside. Thus when the Farningham Loyal Sons of the Darenth Lodge of the Independent Order of the Manchester Unity of Oddfellows celebrated their first anniversary in July 1846, they marched to Eynsford and back preceded by 'Hollands' celebrated band'; the 1854 Poultry Show, on the other hand, took place to the more sophisticated strains of the Band of the Royal Artillery, playing selections from popular overtures. Large travelling shows, like Wombwell's circus, which attended Farningham fair on a number of occasions in the 30s and 40s, brought their own band of musicians, sadly often drowned out by the noise from lesser shows. More intimately, in the home, this was the day of instrumental duets and solos, of songs accompanied and unaccompanied, of the piano in the

View in the centre of Farningham today: the Lion inn, overlooking the Darent.
On the left, the four-arched 'county' bridge, built in 1773 and widened in 1833, which carried all the London–Maidstone traffic in the days of Marianne Farningham.

parlour, performed on and listened to with pleasure at all social gatherings. Significantly, Marianne Farningham's first published poem was called 'Music in Heaven'.

Local outdoor entertainments, which could be counted on to draw good crowds in the still untimetabled countryside, were Farningham Races, started in the 1830s at the Hop Pole inn and well established by the 40s, as well as the occasional steeple-chase run between Dartford and Farningham, or a pigeon-shooting, also a favourite Hop Pole attraction. There seems to have been little difficulty in attracting a crowd even in the middle of the week, as we learn from *The Maidstone Journal* in April 1840, when,

> On Thursday last, a great number of persons assembled at the Hop-pole race course, Farningham, understanding that a race was to take place between Loud's brown mare Victoria and Mr Charlton's horse Blooms-bury. The match originated the previous week, when the Surrey fox hounds threw off at that spot, and was for £20 a side to run twice round the course, ridden by the owners. Mr Loud being ill was unable to ride, and Mr Charlton claimed forfeit, which was allowed him by the umpires. After the above had been amicably settled, the parties present, determined not to be disappointed in their sport, knocked up *sur le champ* a match for a sweepstake of £2.3s. added, between the above two horses, and Mr Armstrong's mare, of Southfleet: once round the mile and a quarter course. Bloomsbury won easily.

In the 1850s, too, a pack of foxhounds appears to have been kept in the village by Mr Colyer, and the neighbourhood was hunted over regularly. In November 1854, for example,

> Mr Colyer's fox-hounds met at Timberden on the morning of Tuesday last, when a goodly number of well-mounted equestrians from the Darenth Valley and neighbouring hills met at the appointed place.

In the summer months cricket was a popular pastime, and newspapers often carried lists of local fixtures, village against village, masters against men, school against town, etc., as well as reports of some of their results: thus we learn that in August 1842 Farningham's junior team had the pleasure of beating Horton Kirby juniors by 21 runs.

VI

However, one must ask, of a society that was so obviously male-dominated, what did the women do? For many, clearly, the cares of a large family and the worries of a small income combined to provide more than adequate employment. Nevertheless, one finds a certain number of women among the traders. Martha Stockley is the local painter (sign-painter, rather than house-painter) and glazier for many years until joined by her son John. After the death of her husband, Henry, Mary Gregory continues as the village baker. Similarly, Jane Phillips stays on at the Bull after the demise of her husband James in 1849, running this important inn successfully for seventeen years, and it is not unusual to find women running farms, although often in a kind of interregnum between father and young son. Women frequently worked in various branches of the dress trade: thus in the 1851 census, for example, we find Mary Ann Warren and her daughter Louisa, in the village, the one a straw bonnet maker, the other a stays maker. A number of women, Mary Ann Hearn's Eynsford grandmother and unmarried aunts Mary and Ellen among them, were dressmakers. There were usually several women in any one village who were skilled midwives. Women with a little learning and no children ran schools, or, conversely, widowed and with several children to rear, sometimes took in one or two more and made a small school of it. While not all of them had a skill which was good enough to be marketable, they were all expected to be adequate cooks, needlewomen (many made all their children's clothes), and nurses who could run a home and look after a family. For those with no skills who needed to earn a living, there was cleaning, washing, or hawking: Caroline Woodford, a widow of 22, with a 2-month-old baby boy, who was in the workhouse briefly in 1837 on account of poverty, is described as a hawker of threads, while old widow Jones, in the late 1830s, went about selling rabbit skins. A woman might even be found driving the horses for her labourer-husband's plough, out in all weathers on the stone shattery* of the hillside or the black ground of the valley, described in an essay on 'The Farming of Kent' printed in *The Maidstone Journal* in 1846 as 'surly ill-tempered stuff, . . . frequently requiring six horses to get a plough through it'.

On the other hand, women who were not forced to work by grinding necessity usually did not work at all outside the home, or, if they did, it was solely in a voluntary or charitable capacity. Thus, when Miss Waring dies suddenly in 1840 at the age of 48 while out on a Sunday afternoon walk in Farningham Wood, her obituarist in *The Maidstone Journal* can lament only that the poor have lost a good friend in her. No office was left unfilled by her death, in a society where the principal actors were almost invariably men.

---

* Shattery: Kentish dialect word. Here, the loose, friable earth full of broken flints, characteristic of the North Downs.

A further aspect of Farningham life at this time which needs mentioning is its increasing attractiveness to people whose principal business lay in London but yet who preferred to live in the country. From quite early in the century we find people of this type appearing in the locality: Sir Walter Stirling at Shoreham is an obvious example. John Rogers, pastor of the Eynsford Baptist chapel from 1802 to 1840, who lived in Farningham, appears to have been quite frequently in London, perhaps in connection with his work as Secretary of the Kent and Sussex Particular Baptist Association. The Reverend Jonathan Whittemore, a successor of John Rogers, particularly chose the Eynsford chapel for his sphere of action, as it would allow him to spend the middle of each week in London, where he pursued his publishing interests. There is some evidence that the Mr Thomason who regaled the corn-market dinner with song was engaged in publishing both in Farningham and London. William Dray gave his business address as London, not Farningham. This colonisation of Farningham by people whose work was in London is of interest for the dissemination of London ideas in the village, particularly as regards writing and publishing. There is no doubt whatsoever that Marianne Farningham, whose gifts lay in this direction, was much influenced by Whittemore and indeed the small opening which he provided for her was, in time, to allow this 'working woman' to develop a career which would have been almost undreamt of for a woman only a few decades earlier.

*   *   *

Farningham's bright renaissance in the first half of the 1850s was centred chiefly on agriculture – the Darenth Valley Railway was largely intended for the forwarding of agricultural produce from the area to the London markets, and all the stations on the Darenth Valley line would have been equipped to handle agricultural goods. It offered few openings to those not directly involved in it, nor does it appear to have been very long lived. The corn market dissidents, after a few heady years, were reconciled with their Dartford brethren; the West Kent Poultry Show would seem to have bowed out graciously in 1854 with the unfulfilled hope that this would be 'one of the established fêtes d'été of West Kent, and that its projectors will be rewarded with a yearly succession of delightful and well patronised entertainments'; only the stock market was to have an existence that outlived the decade, continuing until the late 1870s. The idea of the little railway proved to be only a dream, and the business activities of William Dray himself came to a sudden end in the early 1860s. It seems worth recording, however, that the energy and enthusiasm which this period put into the land did not in itself go unrewarded: the years 1853 to 1857 saw a national increase of one fifth in the profits from agriculture. Nevertheless, the agricultural scene provided few openings of the kind that the mid-century children were likely to want – and not merely because they happened to be particularly literate. None of Joseph Hearn's surviving children remained in Farningham: they were the forerunners of the great diaspora, the dispersal of the families of England to every corner of the island and beyond.

2

Marianne Farningham's Family Background

Marianne Farningham says wryly of herself in her autobiography, 'I must have been born a Baptist', and this is not far from the truth, as she was the child and grandchild of devout Baptists, all members of the church in Eynsford, a mile or so from Farningham. This had been founded in the late eighteenth century as a Particular Baptist church, that is to say, believing in the baptism of adults (as opposed to the infant baptism practised in the Church of England) and holding the Calvinistic doctrine of predestination. At the beginning of the nineteenth century it had followed the course taken by a number of Particular Baptist churches in becoming a Strict and Particular church, adhering to a more rigid form of Calvinism. This was the 'faith and order' into which Marianne Farningham, as Mary Ann Hearn, was born, although, as she tells us herself, her views had broadened before she was out of her teens. Both her parents were staunch supporters of the Baptist church all their lives. Her grandfather Bowers, on her mother's side, may himself have been of Baptist stock, since he was a member of a Particular Baptist church in Penn, Buckinghamshire, before he came to Kent. Ann Hearn, on the other hand, her father's mother, came of a Church of England family, but joined the Baptists somewhere around the age of 35.

Ann Hearn, born in 1769, appears to have been the eldest child of George and Elizabeth Wallis. This is a very old name in Farningham (and in surrounding villages) going back there to the sixteenth century at least. George Wallis, her father, was the son of another George, and of his wife Jane, who died just two years before her granddaughter Ann was born. Nineteenth-century Wallises in the village are tailors, and it is possible that this craft was of long standing in the family.

In outline Ann Wallis's story is typical of that of many women at that time. She married in 1791, her husband, Thomas West, being the son of another Farningham family, who may have been shoemakers by trade. Thomas and Ann seem to have left the village as soon as they were married and for some time they both disappear from view. In the early years of the nineteenth century, however, Ann reappears in Farningham, almost certainly as a widow, and probably with several young children. A few years later we find her married to an Eynsford man, Thomas Hearn, and before his death in 1816 two more children have been added to her family, Sarah, born in April 1810 and Joseph, born fourteen months later in June 1811. Ann Hearn returned from Eynsford to Farningham in 1819, where she spent the last twenty years of her life, in the small terraced cottage that was to be the Farningham home of Marianne Farningham.

Ann's sister Rebecca, six years her junior, seems to have been an early convert to the Eynsford Baptist church. We find her name heading the list of women signatories to the letter inviting John Rogers to become the church's second pastor in August 1802, and she was to become his wife the following year or early in 1804. When Ann returned to Farningham as a widow there is no doubt that she quickly came to share Rebecca's religious convictions, and her baptism must have taken place fairly soon. We are told in the autobiography that she was baptised in the Darent, and this probably dates the event to 1805 or the spring of 1806 at the very latest, as the new meeting house, with its own baptistery, was opened in the summer of 1806. In July of that year and again in January 1808 Ann West assisted, as was customary, at the birth of a baby to her sister Rebecca: Mary, Rebecca's second child, being born in 1806 and little Rebecca in 1808. Between those dates, however, Ann had changed her name from West to Hearn by marrying Thomas Hearn, of Eynsford.

We know little about Thomas Hearn. He was perhaps also a shoemaker. We know that he was sympathetic to the Baptist cause because in 1806, before the new meeting house was ready, he lent a room to the Baptists for a few weeks, although he was not at that time a member of the church. For March of that year the Eynsford church minutes note the following: 'Mr T Hearn having offered the Use of his Room till our Meeting is built for to worship in, Agreed to accept of the same with thankfulness'. A licence was duly obtained from Quarter Sessions for this purpose. In July the new meeting house was ready, and the minutes contain the entry, 'That the Thanks of the Church be given to Mr Hearn for the use of his Room and that he be offered the gratuity of 10/6'. It was soon after this that Thomas Hearn must have married Ann West, but he did not himself become a member of the Baptist church until early in 1815, a year before his death in August 1816 at the age of 54.

We cannot know with certainty how many children the widowed Ann

Marianne Farningham's grandmother, Ann Hearn.
This old painting on wood, which in *A Working Woman's Life* is entitled 'My Puritan Grandmother', was destroyed in the Blitz in the Second World War.

West brought back to Farningham with her, but it is likely that there were at least three. William Wallis West, a shoemaker in Eynsford, whose death is recorded in the Eynsford Baptist register in 1832 at the age of 39, seems almost certainly, in view of his combination of names, to have been a son of Ann's. He married Mary Elliott, and they had a number of children before his early death: William, born in 1818, Mary Jane, born in 1821, Ann, born in 1823, Rebecca, born in 1825, and Philadelphia and Sarah, born in 1827 and 1831 respectively, who both died as babies.

In a late registration in Dr Williams's Library (the early dissenting 'register office'), entered in 1836 when dissenters were busy making up records which had not infrequently fallen behind, Ann Hearn is given as the grandmother of a little girl, Sarah Bennett, who had been born in 1813. This is a puzzling piece of evidence, because the 'wife's parents' are here entered as Thomas and Ann Hearn, although at the time the wife, Susanna, would have been born, say, in 1791 or 1792, Ann was married to Thomas West. However, it is possible that Susanna's parents were entered as Hearn and not West because she must have lived for some years prior to her marriage in the Hearn household, and perhaps also because her mother's signature would not otherwise have tallied with the 'wife's parents' name.

The unmarried James West, a Farningham man who died in 1826 at the age of 33, may well have been another of Ann's sons. His death is recorded in the Eynsford Baptist church register, and the fact of his coming from the same village and belonging to the same church as Ann Hearn seems to point to a family relationship.

The births of both Sarah and Joseph to Ann Hearn, daughter of George and Elizabeth Wallis, are recorded in the register of the Eynsford Baptist church. We know very little of their early life, but we occasionally find Joseph mentioned in the Farningham church rates book after 1819, along with other village boys, making small earnings by trapping and killing 'vermin' in the churchyard: sparrows at $\frac{1}{2}$d a head, hedgehogs at 4d. Joseph's earnings were modest indeed (9d in June 1819, 3d in July) but doubtless welcome both to him and to his mother. From the minutes of the Eynsford Baptist church we learn that both children were baptised and received into member-ship of the Baptist church in 1828, Joseph in March and Sarah in April.

Thereafter Sarah's lot darkened. She appears to have been working as a servant, quite possibly at the Bull inn, opposite her home, and at the beginning of the following year she gave birth to a son, James, of whom the landlord of the inn, George Mandy, acknowledged paternity, reimbursing the parish with the cost of Sarah's confinement and the small sums paid weekly in relief for her and her child. Her connection with the Baptist chapel may well have been suspended as soon as her pregnancy was revealed, although there is no entry to this effect in the minutes – perhaps to spare family feelings: she was, after all, the pastor's niece. Small dissenting communities of this kind were very strict not only in their religious observances but in their moral code, and reports of infringements such as drunkenness, working on the sabbath, singing at feasts, playing cricket, even family rows, were regularly investigated and, if found to be true, reproved. The birth of a child to an unmarried girl was of course severely reprobated, even when, as here, the girl must have been the victim. James' birth is not recorded in the Baptist register, but there is an entry in Farningham parish register of his baptism according to Church of England rites some ten months after his birth. Sarah, however, seems to have been accepted back into the Baptist fold in due course, since she was buried at the Eynsford chapel when she died, at the early age of 40.

Joseph, by this time, was probably already apprenticed to a shoemaker, quite possibly to his own step-brother, William Wallis West, in Eynsford, or to another Hearn, Richard, who was also a shoemaker there. Hearn seems to have been a relatively common name in the area at this time. Marianne Farningham disclaims any relationship with some of the Eynsford Hearns, but it seems unlikely, if records were complete, that a distant relationship would not be found between them. By Christmas 1833, when Joseph married Rebecca Bowers, he was out of his apprenticeship and working as a shoemaker in Farningham at the back of his mother's cottage. When he had become established he seems to have taken over the tenancy from her – the whole row of cottages, of which Ann Hearn's was one, was owned by John Rogers – as we find the rates entered in his name from 1836. Ann Hearn, however, continued to live with her youngest son and his family until her death in November 1839 at the age of 70.

This event was commemorated by her sister, Rebecca, with some verses which she copied into an album kept by her daughter Isabella. These appear to have been taken from the first issue of *The Temperance Journal*, with a word altered here and there to make them applicable to Ann. They begin:

Oh! noble and firm was the patriot feeling
    That dwelt in the depths of this true Christian's heart;
Old age could not chill her pure mind from revealing
    Its firmness and vigour, to choose the 'good part'.

The fears of the selfish, the sneers of the scornful,
    Exerted their doubts and their malice in vain;
She looked on the world, and her spirit was mournful
    To see the foul brand of our national stain.

'Do I love' she enquired, 'relations and neighbours,
The cause of the Lord, and the land of my birth?
Oh, then let me join in benevolent labours
To spread true sobriety over the earth.'

Ann Hearn, like her son and granddaughter after her, was clearly a firm
teetotaller, – although there is no evidence, as Marianne Farningham
suggests, of so eminent a temperance campaigner as Father Mathew visiting
the village.

George Bowers, Marianne Farningham's maternal grandfather, was obviously a man of ability and intelligence. He was born in High Wycombe,
in Buckinghamshire, and seems to have migrated from Penn, in that county,
to Farningham in 1805 and thence, in 1808, to Eynsford. He was a
papermaker and engineer who made an excellent impression on the Eynsford
chapel community from the beginning. The Eynsford Baptists were in the
process of planning their new meeting house, and in November 1805, even
before George Bowers' letter of dismission (which served the purpose of a
kind of character reference) had been received from the Penn chapel, George
had been chosen 'to be part of the Committee for Building the Meeting'.
Thereafter the church seems to have leant heavily on the considerable abilities
which George Bowers brought to the community. In February 1807 he was
appointed both to look after the meeting house (with Brother Ford) and
(with Brother Dickins) to audit the deacons' accounts. Later the same year
he was himself 'unanimously chosen to be a Deacon and accepted the same'.
By 1814 we learn that he had 'frequently spoken from the word to several
to their satisfaction in different Villages around', and it was therefore resolved
'that Bro' Bowers be requested to exercise among us on a Monday Evening'.
George Bowers appears to have served the church faithfully to the end, not
infrequently taking services when the pastor was unable to do so. There are
records of a number of funerals conducted by him both at the Old Burying
Ground at Crockenhill and at Eynsford.

George Bowers was nearly 90 when he died, being buried at Eynsford in
June 1859. Although he was not at home on the night of the 1841 census,
we find him there in 1851, aged 81 and still described as a paper-
maker/engineer He would appear to have met his wife, Mary, a daughter
of John and Mary Gibbons, during the course of his migration southwards
from Buckinghamshire (a migration which seems to be a feature in the lives
of several other Eynsford and Farningham people in the early nineteenth
century). Mary, who appears in both censuses, was nearly 70 in 1851, when
she is described as a dressmaker, who had been born in Bermondsey. She
was to live until August 1855 and she, too, lies buried at Eynsford.

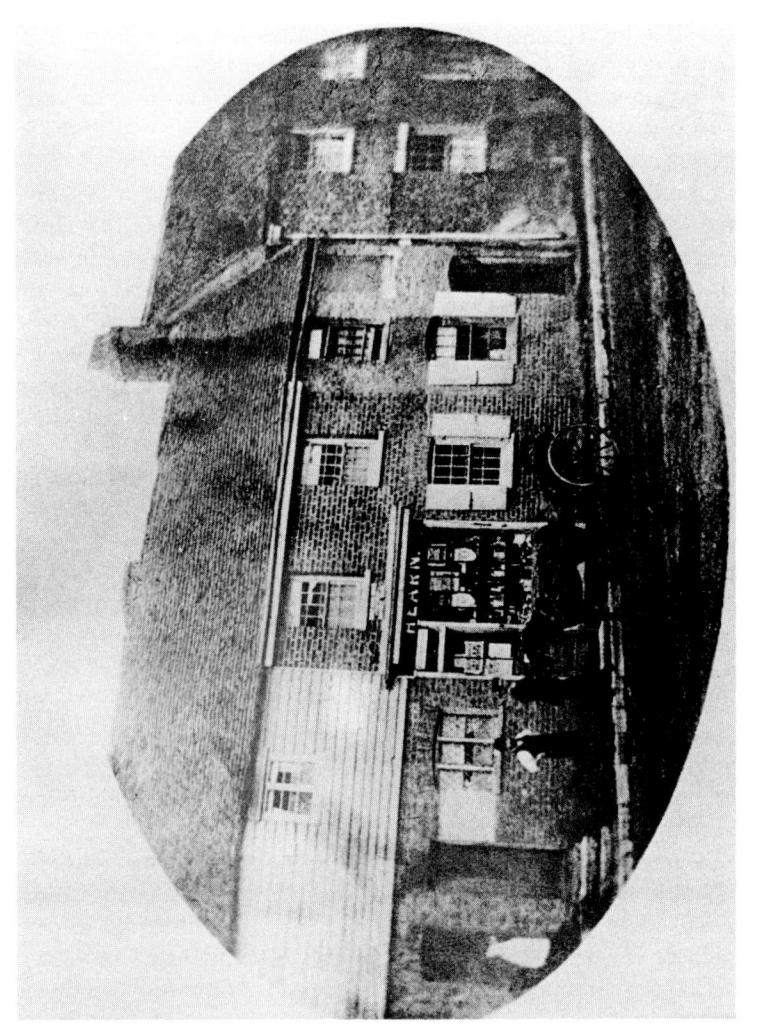

The house in which Marianne Farningham was born and grew up, opposite the Bull inn, photographed some time after she had left home. It is still standing today, very little changed.

Most of the 'large number of sons and daughters' mentioned in the autobiography who lived in the old house 'down the lane' (the Bowers did in fact live in Mill Lane) had left home by the time of the more detailed census returns of 1841 and 1851, although the register of the Baptist chapel gives us the names of some of Polly Hearn's Bowers aunts and uncles, including Sarah, John, Mary, Henry, William, Ann and Ellen. 20-year-old Ann (she was in fact 23) is shown at home with her mother in 1841, while in 1851, when the Bowers also have a lodger in Alicia Bamford from Leicester, the 29-year-old mistress of the Eynsford British School with whom Mary Ann Hearn was shortly to go to Bristol to teach, we find Ellen there, aged 27. The occupation of both Ann and Ellen is given as 'dressmaker', a skill which they had no doubt learnt from their mother, but there is some evidence to show that Ellen may have branched out by 1860 and become involved in the running of the Metropolitan Female Printing Office in Salisbury Square, off Fleet Street, where the compositors were all women, and which was responsible for printing Marianne Farningham's first book of poems, *Lays and Lyrics of the Blessed Life*.

Marianne Farningham herself sketches in briefly the story of her parents. They were married in Farningham in 1833, when Joseph was 22 and Rebecca 21, on Christmas day, a holiday and therefore a convenient time for a wedding. The short ceremony, which was performed by the curate, the Reverend Burnside, took place in the parish church, since it was not until some 3 years later that dissenters were allowed to be married in their own place of worship. The wedding was attended by several of Rebecca's brothers and sisters – John, Mary, Henry, William and Ann – and also by Joseph's sister, Sarah, all of whom signed the parish register as witnesses, with Joseph and Rebecca. Then Joseph took his young bride back to his mother's cottage in Farningham, where all five of her children were to be born, and which was to be her home for the rest of her life.

The details given about Joseph Hearn in the census would seem to imply that his affairs as a shoemaker throve steadily: in 1841 he is shown with 2 apprentices; by 1851, when he is given as a boot-maker and master, he is employing 4 men and has one apprentice. However, Farningham seems never to have had fewer than four shoemakers over this time, and in order to help maintain his steadily growing family – by 1841 there were four small children, Mary Ann, who was 6, Rebecca, 4, Alfred, 3, and Hephzibah, 1, and a fifth, Thomas, was to be born in 1842 – and to support his mother, Joseph Hearn took on another occupation, that of village postmaster. From the parish rates books we find that between 1839 and 1842 he was occupying not only his mother's cottage, but also the cottage next door, where until then Ann Clements (of whom the Reverend Burnside noted in 1838 that she was

'scarcely compos.') had been running the post office. The plan of occupying
the two cottages in tandem seems to have been dropped abruptly in 1843,
when the hard times of the 1840s started to make themselves felt, but Joseph
Hearn appears to have continued to run the post office from his own home.
This was no more than a 'receiving house', to which the post was brought
on foot from Dartford each morning for many years, and where it was
collected in the evening. Joseph Hearn was by no means unusual in having
two occupations: there is plenty of evidence of receiving houses being run
in the middle years of the century by people who also had a trade, like
Joseph Hearn: shoemaker, butcher, tailor, corn-factor, are just a few of the
callings one finds combined with running a local post office.

A later chapter of the autobiography is called simply, 'My Father', and
contains the following appreciation of him:

> The love and joy of my father's life was centred in Eynsford chapel.
> He never missed a service which it was possible for him to attend, and
> the years were crowded with small ministries, always rendered without
> ostentation. He never had much money to give. I think he would have
> given it all to the cause if he had. He was not a good speaker, so he
> was never a very prominent man at the meetings, but he did all that he
> could year after year with unchanging fidelity. My first recollections of
> him in connection with the chapel are, that when I was a very little
> child and grew sleepy in our cosy curtained pew by the door on Sunday
> evenings, I used to rouse up twice during the service to watch my father
> go steadily down the aisle and snuff the candles. I wondered if he would
> not some time snuff one out, but practice had made him adroit in the art.

In describing her father's character Marianne Farningham admits that he
was not altogether a good-tempered man, 'yet he was very clever at making
other people so'. He was, she says, 'known among the Eynsford chapel folk
as "the Peacemaker". He was good at pouring oil on troubled water, and
bringing reconciliation to those who were at enmity. . . . He loved harmony
of all kinds, the wind among the wheat-ears, the whisper of the trees, the
song of birds on the hedges. He delighted in singing. When we were all at
home what times we had over the singing of hymns and songs!' As a young
man Joseph Hearn was already a teacher in the Sunday school, and when
he was 28 he was elected a deacon of the church. In time he rose to be senior
deacon, a position previously occupied by his father-in-law, George Bowers,
and only vacated by Joseph Hearn when he went to live with his journalist
daughter in Northampton in 1879. He had in the meantime married again
– in the 1871 census we find him running Farningham Post Office, with his
wife Sophia – and it seems to have been on the death of his second wife that

it was decided he should move up to Northampton. He married for a third time in Northampton, but did not survive long after that, dying in 1889.

The story of the all too brief lives of Marianne's mother and of her sister Rebecca is told in the autobiography, and nothing can be added to it here. Hephzibah remained in Farningham for about ten years after her marriage to Thomas Sharwood, where he combined the work of tailor and newsagent. In 1871, however, they too moved to Northampton with their family of seven children (they were to have ten in all, five girls and five boys).

Tom, Marianne's surviving brother, also moved eventually to Northampton, and in the 1880s he went out to South Africa with Thomas Sharwood, where he died in 1888. He appears occasionally in Marianne Farningham's writing for children as 'Uncle Tom' or 'Uncle Thomas', a teasing but kindly uncle to various nephews and nieces. He had married Elizabeth Campion, an early suffragette, and left two children, a son Geoffrey, who became a headmaster, and a daughter Margaret, a singer, who was known as Madame Margaret Hearn.

In the year that Tom Hearn died Hephzibah had been sent a ticket to join her husband in South Africa, and she went, accompanied by two of her sons. When she returned in 1891 she was suffering from heart disease, and she was to die two years later at the age of 53. Thomas Sharwood had in the meantime made and lost a fortune in diamonds, and he returned home a poor man – as family tradition had it, 'with a parrot and a bunch of bananas'. Two of Hephzibah's daughters, Elizabeth and Pat, both worked with Marianne Farningham on *The Sunday School Times* for some years, although Pat eventually joined her sisters Alice, Minnie and Marie (Madge) who had emigrated to South Africa, and her two brothers, Harold and Sid, who had stayed on there after their mother's return. Hephzibah's two eldest sons, John and Frank, remained in England, John becoming a house decorator and Frank a boot and shoe manufacturer in Rushden. Frank, a cheerful, lively man, philanthropist and County Councillor, who was himself the father of a large family, is commemorated with a plaque at Rushden Hospital, where he was for many years chairman of the Hospital Committee. He was one of the relatives who was with Marianne Farningham as she lay dying at Barmouth, and it was to him, rousing for an instant from unconsciousness, that she spoke what were perhaps her last words: 'It is the end, Frank. It has been a long day, and a beautiful one, but it is over'.

3

Eynsford Baptist Chapel and its Members

I

The Baptist chapel which meant so much to Marianne Farningham throughout her childhood and youth – and which, indeed, was the great formative
influence in her life – was situated in Eynsford, about a mile south
of Farningham. The first members of the church appear to have migrated
there from Wilmington in about 1792, the year in which the church minutes
begin. These describe it as 'The Particular Baptist Church of Jesus Christ,
Late of Wilmington', and state firmly, 'Form'd June 10th 1792 and Br Morris
Call^d to be our Minister'. The date of 1775 which Marianne Farningham
gives for its foundation would appear to be that of its formation in
Wilmington. This view is supported by the account of the church given in
a small anonymous booklet, *A Short History of the Eynsford Baptist Church*,
which was published around 1905, probably as part of a fund-raising exercise
for the new chapel which in 1906 replaced the early nineteenth century one
that Marianne Farningham had known. Migrations of this kind were not
altogether uncommon: the Baptist church at Bessels Green, for example,
appears to have moved there from Orpington around the beginning of the
eighteenth century.

The first minuted entry for the Eynsford church is as follows:

> Br Morris was Call^d by us and Accepted the Call
> & Placed over us as our Pastor, B^r Britten Pastor of
> a Church Meeting in Hope Street London witness(ed)
> our Order and Preached
> Present Edward Hodges Sam Carter Sam Tovey Wm Brown
> Thos Burberry James Granger

and the first baptisms, which were those of Thomas Burberry, Samuel Tovey
and James Granger, appear to have taken place in October 1793. Samuel

Carter, Edward Hodges and Sarah Cook were baptised in the following July, and the church seems thereafter to have become firmly established in the village, acquiring more members and finding it necessary by 1800 to appoint two deacons in the persons of, first, Edward Hodges and then Thomas Burberry to assist the pastor.

As was required by the Toleration Act of 1689, a certificate had to be obtained from Quarter Sessions, licensing the building or buildings in which the church held its meetings. We can see from these that for some years the Eynsford church did not have a permanent home. In 1799 no less than three places were licensed for its meetings: the houses of Edward Hodges and Richard Lever in March and April respectively, and then, in June of the same year, a building belonging to Samuel Hodsele. It seems very possible that Hodsele's was the building held on a seven year lease, which the church was able to give up when the new meeting house was built. The record for September 1804, which minutes the resolution to collect subscriptions for a new meeting house – frequently termed simply 'the Meeting' – describes the old building as 'too small – very inconvenient, having no Vestry – the Lease but short – & so decayed that without much expence it will fall'.

The new meeting house was one of the first fruits of the energy and enthusiasm of the church's new pastor, John Rogers, who succeeded John Morris in 1802 and who was described at the time as 'late of the Kent Itinerant Seminary, and member of the baptized Church of Christ of the same Faith and Order as ourselves meeting at Walworth Surry'. In Marianne Farningham's autobiography we are given a brief glimpse of John Rogers in his garden, which fronted the turnpike road running through Farningham. Her very slight recollection of him may perhaps indicate that towards the end of his life – he died when she was not quite six – he suffered from illness: the minutes during these years become scanty and are not written in his hand, and we find his son, Henry, conducting a number of services in his place.

Nevertheless, John Rogers' early years had been full of activity: the meeting house with its vestry was opened in 1806, a gallery (which seems to have been used for the Sunday school as well as during services) was installed in the church in about 1812, and both vestry and gallery were later extended. Rogers, who for some years ran his own school in Farningham, where he lived, was clearly interested in education, and a Sunday school was in fact begun at the church as early as the summer of 1802. The first attempt would appear to have failed, and the forlorn little instruction appears in the minutes for March 1806 'that the Hymn Books belonging to the Sunday School be given away at the Discretion of our pastor', but another attempt was made, this time with lasting success, at the beginning of 1808. The membership of the church expanded considerably under John Rogers, and the number of

The first Baptist chapel in Eynsford, built in 1806.

deacons was increased to four and then to five. The 'old burying ground' at Crockenhill was acquired from the Bessels Green church in 1802, and the ground surrounding the church at Eynsford, the whole of which plot seems originally to have belonged to Rogers, was also laid out for burials. The chapel at Crockenhill was at this time being run in conjunction with the Eynsford chapel and this, too, was improved and extended.

John Rogers became in 1806 the scribe or secretary of the Association of Particular Baptist Churches of Kent and Sussex, a post which he held for many years. He seems also to have been a fairly frequent visitor to London. The engravings of him which appeared occasionally during his lifetime show a man with an urbane, slightly quizzical air and a florid complexion, more reminiscent, to our eyes, of the eighteenth than the nineteenth century.

The long pastorate of John Rogers, who was interred, at his own wish, in a vault created out of the old baptistery in the church, was followed in 1840 by an interregnum of two years while the church set slowly about finding itself a new leader. The first choice was not a happy one: George Whitbread, coming with reservations and conditions in 1842 ('I find much retirement essential to my own soul's prosperity and unless I can be much alone I shall suffer and you will also suffer . . . My dear Partner also is unable to bear the fatigue and excitement of frequent visiting any more than myself and the charge of her little family is quite as much as she can properly attend to, even when in health. Do not then expect us often to take our meals from home . . .') resigned in 1845 on the first hint of criticism by 'an influential Party in the Church', but remained in the neighbourhood for over a year, conducting services with a small band of dissidents in the newly-erected British School which was connected with the church.

Stability did not return to the Eynsford Baptist church until 1846, with the appointment of the pastor who appears on more than one occasion in the pages of Marianne Farningham's autobiography, the Reverend William Reynolds, a comparatively elderly man with a young wife and family, who remained at Eynsford for five years. The minutes of the church, as noted down by him, are curiously at variance with the religious enthusiasm of the time – both her own and that of the other members – as remembered by Marianne Farningham. Reynolds, on the contrary, makes repeated reference to 'the low state' of the church, by which he seems to have been referring both to numbers and to income. That the latter weighed heavily with him is proved by his departure in 1851 on account of the meagreness of the salary which the Eynsford church was able to offer him. More than anything else, however, this would seem to reflect the difficult times through which local people were passing – and to which Marianne Farningham herself refers.

William Reynolds' replacement by Jonathan Whittemore in 1852 gave the church the charismatic leadership it had clearly been seeking since the loss of John Rogers. Whittemore who, like Rogers and Reynolds before him, also lived in Farningham, and quite possibly in the house previously occupied by the Rogers family, made no secret of the fact that his choice of Eynsford and Farningham was based mainly on the ease with which he could travel up to London each week, to pursue his publishing interests, although he was attracted, too, by the beauty of the Kentish countryside. Whittemore came to Eynsford from Rushden where, during a peaceful ministry of twenty years, he had had the leisure to bring out a number of publications, among them *The Standard Tune Book*, and to start *The Baptist Messenger*. During his time in Eynsford he was to found the two papers with which Marianne Farningham was to be associated for the rest of her life, *The Christian World*, and *The Sunday School Times*.

The Christian World was begun in 1857 as *The Christian World and General Intelligencer, containing the News of the Week*, with the perhaps over-ambitious aim of 'Forming a Religious, Literary, Educational, Philanthropic, Commercial, Agricultural and Family Journal and Advertiser'. But it was above all a serious attempt, and apparently a very successful one, to bring some unity and amity to the various nonconformist denominations, and its 'Chronicle of the Churches', a regular feature which also covered the Church of England, was valuable in promoting understanding on all sides. The paper bore the motto, 'In things essential, unity; in things doubtful, liberty; in all things, charity'. In her autobiography Marianne Farningham makes the following comment on the paper and its founder:

> Was it strange that one of the pioneers in this crusade of toleration was the minister of a church founded on the doctrines of predestination and election, whose members believed there were few who should be saved, and who refused the Lord's Supper to all believers who had not been immersed? I think not. Extremes provoke revolt.

The Sunday School Times was intended for teachers, parents and the older scholars of Sunday schools. A small, eight-page paper which sold for a halfpenny, it was begun by Whittemore in 1860 less than a year before his death.

Whittemore seems to have kept no minutes of church meetings during his Eynsford pastorate, so that we cannot know whether he considered the church to be on the upgrade or the downgrade. However, his drive and his interests opened new doors for perhaps more than one member of the community, and his considerable contributions to Christian journalism, among which must be counted that of helping to set a young village girl on a career which was to make her known, in time, throughout the length and

breadth of England and Wales, will perhaps be thought sufficient atonement
for this sin of omission.

II

From its earliest days Eynsford Baptist church seems to have been given
considerable encouragement by the paper mill, established in the village some
time during the seventeenth century and later owned by the Johannot family,
who were quite possibly Huguenots. It is difficult to know to what extent
the dissenting Huguenot tradition (if it existed) was continued in the mill,
for by the end of the eighteenth century this was under new owners, John
Floyd and John Fellows. Nevertheless, there is evidence that the Baptists
were given strong support by both partners, particularly by John Floyd and
his wife, who each left a legacy to the church. Floyd, dying in 1804, left £20
'for the support of the Gospel', and he is described in the church minutes
as 'a constant Hearer with us'; his widow, who died in 1819, bequeathed 19
guineas to the church. John Fellows was voted the thanks of the church in
1806 'for lending us his Premises for some time past to administer the
Ordinance of Baptism in' – obviously part of the paper mill built over the
clear waters of the Darent. There is no doubt that many of the early adherents
of the little church worked in the mill: Edward Hodges, who later removed
to St Mary Cray, but lies buried at Eynsford, is described as a papermaker,
as is faithful Samuel Tovey, a papermaker journeyman, who appears to be
the only one of those first named in the minutes to survive, with his wife
Betty, into the 1841 census at Eynsford. Tovey, who died in 1846 aged 79,
is given an affectionate obituary in the minutes, where he is described as 'the
last surviving member of those who first composed the Church at Wilmington'.

It is not possible to analyse the membership of the chapel in any detail,
as there are no full lists of members over the first half of the nineteenth
century. Membership was by no means restricted to the paper mill, however,
nor to the 'small tradesman' class which is so frequently assigned to such
churches, but seems to have included people from many walks of life. The
following list of those named as trustees of the meeting house in 1822 shows
the variety of callings of those in sympathy with its aims, as well as the wide
radius from which the church drew its support:

William Hardyman Colyer, gentleman, of Foots Cray
John May, farmer, of Foots Cray
William Atwood, shopkeeper, of Farningham
Thomas Turner, baker, of Farningham
William Wallis West, shoemaker, of Eynsford
Robert Wilson, miller, of Eynsford
John Whitehead, papermaker, of Eynsford
Edward Crowhurst, shoemaker, of Shoreham
Richard Elliott, farmer, of Swanley
William Crowhurst, farmer, of Ash
Richard Bishop, smith, of Ash
James Turner, baker, of Crayford
John Allwork, cooper, of Sevenoaks
William Ring, baker, of Sevenoaks
William Rogers, house agent, of Walworth.

In 1838 Farningham's curate, the Reverend Andrew Burnside, made his own census of the parish, noting down, among other things, the religious affiliations of his parishioners. This is useful in showing the strength of dissent in a Kentish village which, while not having its own nonconformist chapel (the Wesleyan Methodist chapel in Farningham was not established until 1850) was close enough to be influenced by that of Eynsford, only a mile away. Out of the 150-odd households listed by the Reverend Burnside, some 16 are given as dissenting, while an almost equal number is given as never at church, or as attending no place of worship.

The dissenting families in Farningham in 1838 were those of the following: William Atwood, a grocer and draper, who was also agent for the Norwich Union Fire Insurance Society; John Bath, a market gardener; Joseph Beckley, whose wife kept a day school and who had become the local assistant registrar following the 1836 Registration Act; William Crockford, a farmer; John Gibson, a carpenter; William Gibson, a blacksmith; Joseph Hearn (Marianne Farningham's father), a shoemaker; James Phillips, a farmer; John Rogers, who was himself the minister of the Eynsford Baptist chapel; Thomas Turner, a baker. In addition, a number of single people were also stated to be dissenters: William Hardyman Colyer, of independent means; George Le Feuillade, a cabinet maker; Miss Petersen; Widow Phillips; Widow Tidman; Widow Yates. Not all of these were totally committed to the cause: Mr Burnside noted that Miss Petersen and James Phillips sometimes came to church; Joseph Beckley and his wife oscillated between the two, although both finally came to rest in the small graveyard surrounding the chapel; John Bath, a supporter of dissent for many years and several of whose relatives, including his nine-year-old daughter Elizabeth, are interred in the Old Burying Ground at Crockenhill, himself lies in the churchyard of Eynsford parish church. George Le Feuillade, who was only in the village for a few years, was censured, and possibly disowned, by the chapel for failing to live up to the high moral demands which were made of its members.

Apart from the occasional act of hooliganism, such as is described after the baptism of Ann Hearn in the Darent, there is little evidence of dissenters being persecuted in the village, and dissenters who were in trade were certainly not boycotted on account of their faith, since it is clear that the dissenting community was not, on its own, big enough to support them. On the contrary, we find, for example, that William Atwood the grocer was regularly asked by the parish vestry to provide 'Sundry Articles' for the poor – clothing, as well as such things as mops and brooms for the poor house – all of which were paid for out of the parish poor rates.

Marianne Farningham comments on the great distances which many members of the Baptist church travelled each Sunday in order to take part in its services, and this was undoubtedly one of the distinctive features of such churches. The lack of other Baptist churches in the area was largely the reason for this, although there was a certain amount of hiving-off from established churches such as that at Eynsford. Brother Anthony Smith, for example, in 1810, requested permission to set up a church at Crayford on the grounds of distance; some Hadlow members left to form part of a new church at Hadlow in 1825; in 1832 there was a large secession of Meopham members, who by their own wish were formed into a separate church at Meopham; in 1841 20 members left to form a church at Sutton-at-Hone. These very secessions, however, illustrate the far-flung appeal, either of the church or its pastor, over time and distance.

It is difficult to know the personal reasons which led individuals to become converts to the dissenting chapel, but there are a number of instances of single women and widows turning to it, both young and old. John Rogers' wife, Rebecca (who was a member of the church before his arrival in 1802) came of an old Church of England family, the Wallises, none of whom, except for her sister Ann (on being widowed) appears to have followed her lead. Louisa Sawkins, a daughter of the Shoreham paper mill owner, Thomas Wilmot, joined the Baptists after returning to her native valley on the death in Norwich of her husband Dansie. There is no doubt, however, that a dissenting chapel such as that at Eynsford, responsible for its organisation only to itself, offered a somewhat different social climate from that of the Church of England.

The Eynsford Baptist church formed a community in which the less affluent members of society were not thereby permanently incapacitated, whatever their skills, from acquiring leading positions in it. It is quite inconceivable, for example, that George Bowers the engineer/papermaker and Joseph Hearn the shoemaker, of whom his daughter states explicitly that he 'never had a yard of land of his own' (and the same would seem to be true of George Bowers) could ever have become churchwardens (the equivalent of deacons) in the established churches in Eynsford and Farningham, positions which were regularly held by the most well-to-do, frequently large farmers, in the parish. A church such as the Eynsford Baptist church, on the other hand, offered its members positions of responsibility as deacons, trustees of the meeting house, members of building committees, auditors of accounts, messengers to annual association meetings, Sunday school superintendents and teachers, which would have been largely out of their reach – and indeed, most of which were not required – in the established church. It also seems quite possible that the nonconformist churches were welcoming women as Sunday school teachers before the established church saw fit to accept them. The Baptist church, too, occasionally put them on committees: in 1818 we find Sisters Atwood, Bowers and Turner nominated with Brothers Gooding and W. Elliott to solicit subscriptions to liquidate the debt incurred by enlarging the meeting house. In many ways these small self-governing churches were democratic units when democracy, by the country at large, was still regarded with more than suspicion. As early as 1807 deacons were being elected by ballot, and in their church meeting the members appear to have had a considerable say in the running of their own church. There can be no doubt, therefore, that nonconformist churches like the one at Eynsford were *per se* more democratic than the established church, and also that they offered considerably wider opportunities for lay participation.

4

Education in Marianne Farningham's Family

Marianne Farningham's intense desire for learning runs like a bright thread through the early chapters of her life. It was a longing which was never fully assuaged, for she went to school only in snatches, with what appears to have been a brief attendance at a dame school when she was very young, followed at the age of nearly ten by a few years of more regular schooling, although even this was not unbroken. For further education she received only a few weeks' training as an infant teacher, at the Home and Colonial College in London.

There was clearly a strong tradition of literacy on both sides of the family. Both Marianne Farningham's parents were fully literate, a fact vouched for by their having been teachers in the Baptist Sunday school. It is clear, too, that each came from a literate background: when they married in 1833, a time when parish marriage registers are still full of the X's which denote non-writers, their marriage entry contains only signatures, from Bowers and Hearns. Rebecca's father, George Bowers, was a skilled artisan who was both literate and articulate, and there can be no doubt that his local preaching and the religious debate into which he entered with spirit, and which Marianne remembers listening to in her kitchen, were fuelled by considerable reading. His wife, Mary, a dressmaker, appears also to have been fully literate, entering her name and qualification on little Mary Ann's certificate of registration in Dr Williams's Library in a neat clear hand.

There is no doubt about the literacy of Joseph Hearn's mother, Ann Hearn, whose signature also appears on the Dr Williams's certificate: it was she who taught Mary Ann to read, although she was to die before her little pupil was quite five. Marianne describes her grandmother and her grandmother's sister, Rebecca Rogers, as 'both strong, sweet women, of considerable culture and striking mental powers', and the question arises of where, in the eighteenth century, they would have acquired an education which was to prove so hard to come by in the nineteenth.

Educational provision of the time seems to have included a considerable

No. *1297*   258

Dated the *11th* day of *July* 183*6*

This is to certify and declare, that

Mary Ann Hearn the *daughter*

of *Joseph Hearn*

of *Farningham* in the *County*

of *Kent Shoemaker*

and *Rebecca Hearn* his wife (who was

the daughter of *George & Mary Bowers*

of *Eynsford* in the *County*

of *Kent*) was born at the house

of *the said Joseph Hearn*

in *the Parish of Farningham*

in the *County* of *Kent*

on the *seventeenth* day of *December* 183*4*

Joseph Hearn
Rebecca Hearn } The Parents abovenamed.

‡ *Mary Bowers Grandmother of the Child*

We certify and declare that we were present at the Birth of the Child above-
mentioned; and that such Birth took place at the time and place aforesaid.

† *Hunt. Surgeon* of *Farningham*

† *Ann Hearn.* of *Farningham*

Received, Filed, and Registered, *according to the custom in use
among Protestant Dissenters, at the Registry of Births kept at
Dr. Williams's Library, Red-Cross Street, Cripplegate, London,
this* *25th* *day of* *October* 183*6*.

By me, *Richard Cogan*

REGISTRAR.

The certificate of birth of Mary Ann Hearn (Marianne Farningham) filed at the Dissenting Registry of Births at Dr Williams's Library in 1836.

number of very tiny establishments, consisting frequently of no more than an educated lady or gentleman (the gentleman often in Holy Orders) who took two or three pupils, usually as boarders. We find education of this type being advertised until well into the middle of the nineteenth century. Thus in *The Maidstone Journal* for July 1848 we find 'A Lady' advertising for 'Two Little Girls to Board and Instruct in the usual routine of an English education. They would, while their health, manners, morals, were carefully attended to, enjoy all the comforts of home'. In June 1852 we read, 'A Lady, a Member of the Church of England, residing in the neighbourhood of Gravesend, Kent, who undertakes the care of six Young Ladies, would be glad to hear of some, to fill up vacancies', while in January 1854 a note of professionalism is creeping into this advertisement from the Tunbridge Wells area:

> Infants' Home – A Teacher from the 'Home and Colonial', with ten years' experience, is anxious to obtain the care of Two Little Boys Under Six, or Girls Under Nine Years of Age. She offers a very comfortable home and education in the strictest sense, on most moderate terms. No holidays unless required.

The 1848 advertisement actually mentions terms, which the others do not: £22 a year if under 8 years, £24 for 8 to 12 years. It seems unlikely, however, that a village tailor would have been able to pay out sums of this order for the education of his daughters. The fact that neither Ann nor Rebecca married particularly well seems also to cast doubt on their having received a 'lady's' upbringing. It appears more likely that the tailor's family would have taken advantage of any local facilities which were available.

We know that Farningham had a school throughout the second half of the eighteenth century, from details contained in several religious surveys which were made during this time. Archbishop Secker's *Speculum* of 1758–1768 describes Farningham as having 'A large private School for Reading, Writing and Arithmetick', while Archbishop Moore's Visitation Returns of 1788 elicit from the then vicar, John Saunders, the information that 'There is a good School, but not a Charity one', with the additional note that 'Some poor Children are sent to it by some of the Inhabitants'. In 1807 the Reverend William Van Mildert's report on the state of his parish of Farningham, made in response to the Visitation Articles of Archbishop Manners Sutton, speaks of 'a Day School supported by weekly or quarterly payments for the children taught in it, and kept by a reputable Schoolmaster of the Church of England. The number of children (Boys and Girls) is about 70. There is also another smaller school of the same kind, kept by a Schoolmistress of the Established Church; the number of children about 20'.

Van Mildert's entry is particularly valuable in confirming that the principal school was a mixed one. It does not seem unreasonable to infer, therefore, that Ann and Rebecca Wallis may have received their education in the village school which seems to have had a (possibly unbroken) existence of many years.

Wherever the Wallis sisters were educated there is no question of their resulting ability and cultivation. Unfortunately, although her granddaughter tells us that she wrote poetry, no examples of Ann's work seem to have come down to us. Some of Rebecca's writing, however, is preserved in a family album which belonged in the first place to her daughter Isabella, the one who taught Marianne Farningham to write. The following poem, which was perhaps one of the first entries in the album, is interesting both as an example of the level of attainment which could be met with among the ordinary inhabitants of a village who had received their education before 1800 and also for its description of an earlier way of life. While not great verse, the lines are neatly turned and serve the occasion well enough. They are signed R.R., and were probably written around 1841.

> Dear, how times are altered! why when I was young
> I ne'er saw an Album, the ladies had none.
> To be sure they kept books, which they called common-place
> And were their own scribes, which was sure no disgrace.
> The events of the village they sometimes inscribed –
> When such an one married, when such an one died,
> The fortune of one, or the will of the other,
> What money was left to a friend or a brother.
> To strengthen their memory for conversation
> They sometimes inserted the news of the nation
> That in company they might have something to say,
> Although they thought politics out of their way.
> Then domestic things they would write in their book,
> A receipt for a pudding, from such a nice cook,
> The best way to make a fine pie or a tart,
> And nice little nick-nacks, that required some art,
> With directions for roasting and boiling of meat
> And to set out their table with dishes complete,
> Then how to brew porter, and ale that's so fine
> And of different things to make excellent wine,
> That they with such knowledge good wives might become
> And so make their husbands quite happy at home.
> But should such good living make some of them ill
> They could find in their book a receipt for a pill,

Another for chilblains, and a lotion for burns,
A draught for a fever, and plaister for corns.
But Albums in dresses all edged with gold
Are a new tribe of beggars, and so very bold
That they really become quite a tax on one's brain
For they ransack each corner a scrap to obtain,
Nor yet is this feature the worst in their phiz
For your scrap they'll expose unto many a quiz
Who will laugh at its meanness, and say 'tis too poor
To be placed in an Album – a lady's choice store.

With such a literate grandmother and great-aunt one might have expected little Polly Hearn to be heir to an even greater level of literacy, but such was not in fact the case. The village school referred to earlier was continued in her day as Charles Everest's Weekly School. We do not know what was charged for this, although for some years from 1818 20 children were being sent to it for a fee of £1 per year per child, paid for out of the village's Roper Charity. However, it was not the fee but the creed which kept Joseph Hearn from sending his children there: naturally enough, dissenters' children were not sent to a school which, by inculcating the principles of the established church would have drawn them back to the Church of England. There is no doubt that the nonconformists saw the educational dilemma which this posed for their children, and many of their pastors and ministers attempted to close the gap by running schools themselves: locally one can instance John Stanger at Bessels Green, as well as John Rogers at Farningham. A few dissenting academies certainly attained to national eminence – that of Dr Philip Doddridge at Northampton was one such. But local schools of this kind do not appear to have been very long lived. John Rogers, who for two or three years actually rented a house in Farningham for this purpose, seems to have continued the school thereafter in his own home until all his children had received at least the rudiments of an education. We know, at any rate, from the Reverend Benjamin Sandford's 'Return on Education' in 1819 that Rogers's school at this time had 23 pupils. It seems likely that Sarah and Joseph Hearn, his niece and nephew, who moved to Farningham when they were nine and eight respectively, would have been educated with their cousins, the little Rogers. The system faltered, however, with a pastor's disinclination to continue as a pedagogue, and nonconformists clearly did not have the funds to establish and support schools on the scale of those of the established church: Everest's school, for example, benefited not only from 'charity' children, but from premises provided by the church, in return for the oversight of the Sunday school, and from free coal for heating.

This was the educational gap into which Marianne Farningham fell as a dissenter's child, and which the state left unremedied until 1870, when Forster's Education Act (by imposing a 'conscience clause' on all schools receiving a government grant) solved the religious intransigence of the two principal voluntary educating bodies, the Church of England National Society and the nonconformist British and Foreign School Society. Parents were now permitted, if they wished, to withdraw their children from a school's religious instruction. In addition, Forster's Act ordered the formation of a school board to establish and maintain a rate-aided public elementary school, wherever insufficient provision was offered by the voluntary societies. William Forster himself used the phrase 'filling up gaps', and in the autobiography of Marianne Farningham we do indeed have the testimony of a girl who wasted precious years in just such a gap.

As it was, Marianne's education was rescued, perhaps just in time, by the setting up of a school by the Baptist chapel in Eynsford, under the aegis of the British and Foreign School Society. The schools of this Society had the support of most, if not all, of the nonconformist denominations, Baptists, Quakers, Congregationalists, Methodists and Independents among them. They inculcated no creed or dogma, but taught directly from the Bible, a procedure acceptable to them all. Marianne Farningham was one of the first scholars enrolled, and it was here, in a single-room school typical of the period, 30 feet by 21 feet, built of brick with a slate roof and wooden floor, that she received the major part of her education.

The school seems to have been under a mistress in its early years: Miss Eliza Hearn at first and then, following her departure, Miss Alicia Bamford. Subsequently, that is to say, after Marianne Farningham had left, it may have had a master, George Webb, although he seems to have run the school as a private one for some years – a fact which underlines the school's shaky financial basis.

Teacher training colleges had only made their appearance during the 1830s and 1840s. The Home and Colonial College in the Grays Inn Road, to which Marianne went, was an early one, founded in 1836 to provide training for teachers in infant schools by the Home and Colonial Infant School Society. This had evolved from the London Infant School Society, with which a number of early educationalists and prominent figures concerned with education had been connected, including James Mill, Lord Brougham, Zachary Macaulay and Samuel Wilderspin. Such training colleges were seen to be essential if the new schools which were now springing up in considerable numbers were to do an efficient job. They were funded from a variety of sources, including government grants, but their students seem to have been largely thrown on their own resources when it came to paying fees. While quite often supported by a patron or by their church, for whom they would then return to teach, many were sponsored for no more than two or three months, thus posing, among other things, considerable organisational problems for the new colleges. It is possible that Marianne Farningham received some help in this way from her church, with perhaps a contribution or two from a local benefactor. Even so, she was able to 'buy' no more than a few weeks of training.

Nevertheless, even a brief period of training was more than many teachers could boast at this time: the Diocesan inspection of the National Schools in the Deanery of Shoreham (in which Farningham lay) which was carried out by the Reverend B. F. Smith in 1851, for example, found about half the teachers, both men and women, untrained, while of those who had received some training the length of it varied wildly from 2 months to $2\frac{1}{2}$ years.

It must have been very difficult for Marianne Farningham to absorb the lessons given in this totally new environment over so short a period. Apart from anything else, her head must have been buzzing with new impressions: we know of only one previous occasion, and that a sad one, when she had visited London. Now, the weeks at the Home and Colonial College marked the end of her formal education: after that she was out in the world, imparting to others the knowledge which for her had been so hard to come by.

5

The Working Years: 1857–1909

Although teaching provided a welcome route to independence for many women in the mid-nineteenth century there are indications from Marianne Farningham's early writings both that she would have welcomed the married state and that she was drawn somewhat reluctantly to teaching. She was not in the mould of a Frances Power Cobbe (whom she knew well towards the end of her life), eager to enter the fray of a Ragged School, but rather shy and perhaps somewhat fastidious by nature, and it seems more than likely that the 'horror of dirty, ragged little children' ascribed to the heroine of the story 'For my Saviour' in her first collection of tales and poems, *Echoes from Darenth Vale*, was in fact a horror felt initially by herself.

The first story in this collection, 'The Unknown Way', appears to be based almost wholly on personal experience. The girl's loss of her mother, here, follows so closely the account given in the autobiography of the death of Marianne Farningham's own mother, that there seems little reason to doubt the reality of the other main event in the story, the deeply-felt loss of a boy's friendship, and perhaps even love, caused by the heroine's entering the company of the local Baptist 'saints'. The story ends with marriage nevertheless, although without passion, to a missionary encountered some years later during the course of 'good works'. This, however, was the wistful prospect at 23. The autobiography tells us that Marianne Farningham was engaged at least once after she had moved to Northampton, but 'then and afterwards, I was made to know that the sheltered life of a married woman was not God's will concerning me'.

There are no caveats or quibbles to be entered with regard to her life as a writer, however. One of the later chapters in her autobiography begins:

> When we were all young and merry together, two friends and I used to sing a humorous song, the first line of which was 'I'd be a heditor'. It is curious that two out of the three have been editors for many years, and the other a constant contributor to literature.

Marianne Farningham began making up poetry at a very early age, and writing was clearly the activity in which she found the greatest pleasure. At the age of 32 it was proposed to her that she should become a full-time writer, and her delight was obviously very great to be thus 'set free from teaching in school'. Although she later extended her range to include biography and the editing of some books of poetry, she made her greatest impact as a nonconformist Christian journalist, writing principally for *The Christian World* (and other papers associated with it) which Jonathan Whittemore had founded in 1857 when she was 22, and to which she was one of the original contributors.

In a lively passage in the autobiography she describes how she saw her first contribution to the journal in print, over the name Marianne Farningham:

> On Good Friday, 1857, a party of young people, of whom I was one, set out to walk from Farningham to Foots Cray, a distance of five miles, to attend the annual meeting of the West Kent Sunday School Union. As we passed the road leading to Dartford, our nearest railway station, the omnibus drove by. Mr Whittemore was seated on the top, and he held up a little roll of paper for me to see, and then threw it down. One of the young men caught it, and handed it to me. It was the first number of *The Christian World*. I folded it into a small compass – not a difficult feat, for it was a very small paper – and put it away in my pocket, feeling quite shy and nervous. There it remained unopened for several hours, though I was longing to know whether there was really any bit of my writing in it. After a time, in the secluded part of a lane, I opened it, and saw for the first time the name 'Marianne Farningham' in print. It was by Mr Whittemore's advice that I adopted the name of my birthplace. I had chosen 'Echo', which he did not like, and I had not the courage to use my own surname, for it seemed presumptuous, as I was only a poor village girl. Mr Whittemore thought Marianne Farningham was a well-sounding name. I think so, too.

In 1857, however, Mary Ann Hearn still had ten years of teaching ahead of her. In that year she went as a teacher to Gravesend, where she was at first very lonely, a loneliness broken by visits from her sister and Farningham friends, and by occasional visits home on Sunday – she speaks of 'walking the eight miles that lay between Farningham and Gravesend, because I enjoyed it, and to save the train-fare'. She soon made new friends in Gravesend however and in 1859 moved with one of them, Miss Gordge, to Northampton to teach. She could not know that she was to spend the rest of her life, precisely fifty years, in this Midlands town – Leatherton, as it

T.W.Hunt.Sc.

Marianne Farningham at the age of about 25.
From the engraving which formed the frontispiece to *Lays and Lyrics of the Blessed Life*.

was sometimes called, from the vast numbers of boots and shoes made there
– but her last Sunday in Farningham, before her departure, must have been
a moving one:

> My friends, on my last Sunday at home, in the homely fashion common
> to country Nonconformists, offered special prayers for me in the vestry
> of Eynsford chapel, beseeching God to bless and guide me, and to take
> care of me always.

For six years Miss Mary Ann Hearn was headmistesss of the infant
department at the British school in Northampton – by now, no doubt, more
accustomed to her charges than the young girl who had shrunk from dirty,
ragged little children! The time seems to have been a happy and busy one
for her: as well as teaching (and that also included giving instruction to a
pupil-teacher, for which, as she says, she was hardly qualified) she was also
doing a considerable amount of writing. The proposal from James Clarke,
now proprietor of *The Christian World*, that she should become a salaried
member of the paper's staff, encouraged her to consider moving from
Northampton, but at this point she became deeply involved with the girls'
Bible Class at College Street Baptist church, new work which she found
challenging and which was responsible for keeping her in the town. Although
this was of course a form of teaching, dealing with the older girls who formed
the Bible Class, and whose ages ranged from about 16 to 20, seems to have
suited her and must, indeed, have been somewhat akin to present-day
sixth-form teaching. Marianne also seems to have welcomed the informal
atmosphere of such a class, in which she could be friend and helper as well
as teacher. Appreciation between teacher and girls was mutual, and there
were many tributes to her from women who had belonged to her class when
she finally retired from this work in 1901.

It was as a result of her work with her Bible Class that she became for a
few years a professional lecturer. She had already grown accustomed to
addressing the class, which could number anything from fifty to eighty girls,
when she was asked to read a paper at the Sunday School Union. Her success
with this gave her the confidence to feel that she might be able to contribute
with a lecture to the debate which the subject of women's rights was receiving
at that time. She therefore made arrangements, in 1877, to talk in a few
places on 'The Women of Today', and was very soon inundated with
invitations to deliver her lecture elsewhere. During the next five or six winters
she travelled extensively, in the manner of the times, preparing a fresh lecture
each year. The energy expended by all those who set out on the Victorian
lecture circuit is perhaps not always appreciated today. Marianne Farningham records that during two of the six or seven years in which she

was a visiting lecturer she gave a hundred lectures each winter in a hundred different places – a working woman's life indeed!

The profits from her lectures were always shared with the institution in which she was speaking, but in spite of this, the lecturing enabled her to buy her own house in Northampton, at 12 Watkin Terrace, which overlooked the common at the back. For some years she had been living with her sister Hephzibah who, with her husband and family, had moved to Northampton in 1871, and it had been in her sitting-room on the first floor of Hephzibah's house that she had welcomed her vast Bible Class 'family' to their mid-week meetings. Much later, someone who had been a member of the class and who, with everyone else, had been in the habit of leaving her hat and coat in Miss Hearn's bedroom, realised 'what work somebody must have had to put that bedroom and sitting-room right every week after such a large party!' and, knowing who that somebody would have been, added 'But Miss Hearn's sister was second only to our teacher in her kindness to us'.

Mary Ann Hearn's services to teaching were given public recognition in some measure in 1885 when she became a member of the School Board in Northampton, standing for election as an independent on two occasions, on the first of which she triumphantly headed the poll. An examination of the Minutes of the Board does not show her to have been a particularly prominent member of it, and she herself comments of her time there, 'I was not at all sure that all the members of the Board were glad to have me there – I fancy that most women who occupy public positions with men have the same doubt'. But she was clearly not afraid to make her views known, and was a keen advocate of higher grade schools and of day training colleges for girls. A feminist may regret that, as she states in her autobiography, she was instrumental in having cookery lessons put on to the curriculum for girls – perhaps she was remembering the fun she and her sisters had had as girls in Farningham, baking illicit cakes and tarts for their friends! Marianne Farningham resigned from the Northampton School Board in 1891, but her final words on teachers are to be found in her autobiography:

> I am very glad if I have been able to be of any service to teachers, because, in my opinion, they are the finest, most useful, and least appreciated class of persons in the kingdom.

At the beginning of the year in which she was elected to the School Board Marianne Farningham had become editor of *The Sunday School Times*. The full title of this small paper, which, at a halfpenny, was something of a pioneer in the field of cheap journals (although *The Christian World* itself cost only a penny), was *The Sunday School Times and Home Educator*, and its articles were aimed at both markets. It became popular very quickly, reaching a circulation figure of 25,000 copies during its first year, and it seems to have retained the affection of its readership throughout the whole of the time that Marianne Farningham was in charge of it. She had written regularly for it from the start, and when she became its editor, a post which she held until her death, she continued to write many of the items itself – so much so that she was 'afraid that the readers would have too much of Marianne Farningham' and omitted the name from some of her productions! At the same time she was still writing for *The Christian World*, regularly contributing verses and miscellaneous articles.

All her life Marianne Farningham was a keen traveller. She was very much aware of the need to broaden her own horizons if she was to remain lively and interesting as a journalist, and she travelled widely, mainly, of course, by rail – the London and North-Western line, which served Northampton, being her favourite. Her journeys as a lecturer had the added attraction of extending her knowledge of the British Isles both culturally and socially (as well as bringing her many close friends among some of those who were most active in public life, particularly in the churches). By her own account, she went round cathedrals, walked beside rivers, climbed mountains; she saw biscuits being made at Reading, alpaca at Saltaire, china at Worcester, cutlery at Sheffield, cotton goods in Lancashire, woollen materials in Yorkshire, carpets in Halifax, ships in Sunderland, hosiery at Leicester, lace at Nottingham. She was, too, an early exponent of the benefits to be derived from annual holidays, and it was not long before she contrived a way of taking some of her Bible Class away each year, enjoying the impressions made by such places as Hastings, Ventnor, Llandudno, Ramsgate, Brighton, Douglas, Edinburgh and Barmouth on girls for whom this was the first experience of travel.

She also seized eagerly a number of opportunities of travelling abroad, savouring everything to the full: it was not a young woman who toiled through the late June snow to the St Bernard Hospice, causing considerable anxiety to the friends who had added this unplanned detour to the Swiss holiday which had been undertaken to combat the prolonged effect of a bout of influenza:

> 'I would not have brought you here for five pounds,' said our captain. Half an hour later he put the sum at ten, and I kept going up in value, till at last he said, 'I would not have brought you here for fifty pounds if I could have foreseen this.' Another friend, my neighbour, roused me in another way. He was always ready with remedies, but at last he said, 'Pull yourself together if you can. They charge an awful lot of money for carrying a corpse over these lines, and however expensive it would

be, the Northampton people would never forgive me if I did not take you home to be buried!' We all laughed at that, and the laugh did us good.

Four years earlier she had been given the marvellous birthday present of a visit to Palestine on a Cook's conducted tour, but the memories of this were subsequently overshadowed by the death of the kind friend whose present it had been, who unfortunately contracted typhoid while abroad and died shortly after their return.

Although she was herself quite tough, as is shown by her recovery from smallpox when a child, Marianne Farningham exhibited symptoms of a serious breakdown in 1889, brought on both by the strain of personal tragedies in the previous months, when she had lost first her brother and then her father, and by overwork. For thirty years she had kept up her literary work with scarcely a break, always writing busily for the papers with which she was associated, even when travelling. Now, Messrs Clarke responded at once by forcing a long respite on her, and in order to help her recover her health a friend accompanied her to Italy.

There were no shadows over the Italian visit. The small, indefatigable traveller revived in the Italian sun, hastening from Turin to Genoa, from Naples to Pompeii, from Perugia to Florence, running along an 'interminable' line of omnibuses with the names of their hotels on them until she came to one which looked 'comfortably familiar and English' and bore in big letters the words 'Hotel Smith', climbing the two hundred and ninety-four steps of Pisa's leaning tower, a temperance speaker who found the air of Rome, 'the city of dream and desire', 'positively intoxicating', and wished herself a boy, 'that I might throw up my hat and dance for joy'. Totally ignorant about painting, as she admitted herself, she seems to have been swept off her feet both by Italy's art and by the scenes which inspired it, writing many years afterwards in her autobiography, 'I am afraid that as long as I live I shall not cease to regret that I have not been able to pay a second visit to Rome, with leisure to write my impressions as they came to me'. No wonder that in her later years, at Barmouth, she enjoyed the friendship of John Ruskin.

For many years she had longed for a small country retreat of her own and in about 1886 the dream was finally realised, when she was able to rent a tiny Welsh cottage overlooking the Mawddach Estuary at Barmouth. Her pleasure in the 'little gabled house, situated on a crag at the foot of a mountain, and high up above most of my neighbours' chimneys' and in the views it commanded over mountain and sea, was never diminished. It was here that she fled when the break had to be made with the Bible Class that had been so dear to her, and here, subsequently, that she began and wrote most of her autobiography. Barmouth also enriched her life with the society

Marianne Farningham at the age of 50.
From the photograph which accompanied the announcement in *The Sunday School Times* of her appointment as editor.

of some notable men and women who lived in the area, among them Mrs C. T. Talbot, the owner of her cottage, local benefactress and donor of land to the National Trust, whose friendship also brought her that of John Ruskin and of Frances Power Cobbe, the women's rights worker and anti-vivisectionist.

The last few years of her life seem to have been divided between Northampton and Barmouth, where she now usually spent the winter. In 1901, at the annual May meeting of the Sunday School Union held in Exeter Hall in the Strand, London, she had what she herself described as 'one of the supreme moments of my life', when she was the first person to receive a testimonial for her record of prolonged service to the Sunday School movement. When her name was called, the whole assembly, including a long row of press men and women, rose and gave her a standing ovation. Most of her activity was now in the past although in 1902 she became for two years a co-opted member of the Northampton Education Committee, appointed under the new Education Act. March 1906 saw her in Eynsford for the last time, when she attended as a speaker at the valedictory and centenary meetings held in the old chapel which had been so dear to her. This was probably one of the last large gatherings at which she was present, but she still travelled when she could and during the summer of 1907 spent a month at Bassenthwaite, in the Lakes, holidaying and correcting the proofs of her autobiography at one and the same time.

This had been some six years in the writing. In his short memoir entitled *Marianne Farningham in her Welsh Home*, published a few months after her death, the Reverend W. Glandwr-Morgan, her Barmouth pastor and friend, recalled the struggle she had often had to put her memories on paper:

> . . . it was plain to all of us that the writing of it was costing her much. Often when recounting to us days of early childhood, and her work in Northampton, the tears flowed freely down her cheeks, and she would exclaim, 'I am so unworthy, God has been good to me; I have but little of interest to give out, just a workaday life, yet if it helps another in the daily struggle it will be worth all.' Much of this book was written in the very early morning at Craig-yr-Helbul – sitting up in her bed, with the glories of nature in view.

1907, the year of publication of *A Working Woman's Life*, was the fiftieth anniversary of her association with *The Christian World*, and she was called on to celebrate this both in Northampton and in Barmouth. However, she seems to have been already unwell on the occasion of the Barmouth celebrations, held in the Frances Power Cobbe room of the local library of which she herself was a director, and the ceremony, at which she was presented with a purse of gold sovereigns, had to be curtailed. Her illness became serious, and early in 1908 she was given only a few days to live. However, she made a surprising recovery and the following summer found her again in Barmouth, where she graduated from a bath chair and the level ground of Brongwynedd to making the ascent to her own dear cottage. The winter was spent among her family in Northampton, and here, at the end of 1908, she again became very ill. When March brought a hint of the spring which she so loved, she asked to be taken back to Barmouth and it was there, on the 16th March, that she died peacefully after being unconscious for three days. Her funeral service at the College Street Baptist chapel in Northampton was conducted by the President of the Baptist Union, the Reverend Charles Brown, and she was buried in the Municipal Cemetery in Billing Road, amid honours paid her by the local, national and religious press.

She had kept up her work until the very end: her last poem for *The Christian World* was written only a month before her death, and a seventh collection of her verse, *Songs of Joy and Faith*, containing a selection of poems from earlier collections, as well as more recent work, was brought out posthumously in September 1909.

Her will dispersed among her nephews and nieces and close friends the small treasures of a selfless and public life, including her grandmother's portrait, her father's silver tea spoons, her books, her pictures, her piano, and a low chair which had been given her by her girls' class. Her *Times* obituarist acknowledged someone who had been 'for half a century well known and very popular'; the compiler of the *Dictionary of National Biography* gave just over half a column to the 'daughter of Joseph Hearn, village postmaster, born at Farningham, Kent'.

There is no doubt that Marianne Farningham was a remarkable woman – gifted, intelligent, endowed with a practical common-sense, warm, witty and loving. Although she often described her early self as shy and retiring, her qualities shone out from an early age, bringing her to the attention, in spite of herself, of all with whom she came into contact – her father's prayer, that she should 'find favour', being abundantly answered.

6

Marianne Farningham as a Writer

Marianne Farningham was a prolific and steady writer. In January 1879, nineteen years after its first appearance, *The Sunday School Times* carried her thousandth set of verses for it, a weekly contribution which was usually accompanied by its fellow in *The Christian World* as well as by miscellaneous prose articles – homilies, short essays, stories for children. By 1879, too, she was also using another pseudonym and, as Eva Hope, who remained active for nearly twenty years, producing slightly different work, mainly biographical.

In all, Mary Ann Hearn contributed over forty books to the Victorian literary scene, most of these originating in the poems, articles and stories which had appeared over the name Marianne Farningham in the above two papers. As such they were published (occasionally in collaboration with Hodder & Stoughton) by James Clarke & Co, later of Fleet Street, who took over *The Christian World* in Paternoster Row shortly after Jonathan Whittemore's death in 1860, and their author came to feel, perhaps a little unfairly to herself, that the name 'Marianne Farningham' belonged to Messrs Clarke. When, in 1875, she was asked by a Gateshead publisher, Adam & Co, to undertake some biographical work, she would only agree on condition that she wrote under another name. It seems just possible that she had already made some use of the name selected, Eva Hope, but she was later to describe it tartly as 'about the weakest we could have found'. It was under this name that biographies of several eminent Victorians appeared, including Grace Darling and the Queen herself, the later ones being published by the firm of Walter Scott, of London and Newcastle-upon-Tyne, which had by then taken over Adam & Co.

In her autobiography she dates her first book to 1860. This is indeed the date of the first volume by 'Marianne Farningham' – published not by James Clarke but by Benjamin Lowe, the original publisher of Whittemore's *Christian World*. However, two years earlier a small collection of prose and poetry had appeared under the name Marianne Hearn, entitled *Echoes from*

Darenth Vale: Tales and Truths in Prose and Verse. This had been published jointly by Benjamin L. Green, of Paternoster Row, and her father, who appears on the title-page as J. Hearn, Post-Office, Farningham, Kent. It is a small book, containing six tales and twenty-nine poems, mostly religious in tone, although three of the poems, headed 'Rural Reminiscences', deal with local themes: 'Darenth Vale', 'Queen Elizabeth at Eynsford Priory', and 'The River Darent'.

Several of the types of work which later flowed from the pen of Marianne Farningham are prefigured in this first collection. Here in particular are the moral story, and the devotional and nature poetry. Here, too, is the journalist behind the story-teller, reporting what she sees, and reporting faithfully, for two reasons: the first being that her religious upbringing had bred in her an unswerving regard for truth, which was to give her the directness and simplicity, and perhaps also the spontaneity, of a girl all her life: and the second, which derives from the first, being that she is a writer of very little imagination, her imagination having perhaps been stifled at birth, since she was taught from early childhood that 'making things up' was akin to falsehood, and the novel, that compendium of adult 'made up' things, positively wicked. Only the real was permitted in her world, and when Mr Whittemore, her pastor, tried to widen her focus by giving her Shakespeare and Charlotte Brontë's *Jane Eyre*, it was too late: she could appreciate, but she could not assimilate.

Apart from an earnest didacticism, which overrides considerations of style, this is one of the reasons for her sometimes rather flat prose: an intentness on reproducing faithfully everyday scenes and the often unrhythmic measures of everyday speech, and an inability to contemplate falsifying these for the sake of a more lyrically satisfying representation of them. This is the more surprising because she had an ear for music and metre, as her poetry shows: her first published poem was called 'Music in Heaven', she loved singing and listening to music, and, in her later work, could quote widely from the poets of her time. But poetry had always represented a special case, an exception, existing in its own right almost like the birds and the flowers. Poetry spoke the truth also, but in its own way: it offered her a tongue, while in prose she had to use her own.

Nevertheless, with both prose and poetry she was addressing a very large audience: less than ten years after it had been started *The Christian World* had a weekly circulation of over a hundred thousand, and this figure was to increase. Many of its readers no doubt came from a background similar to hers and shared many of her views, and for them the qualities which irradiated her writings more than compensated for a somewhat limited prose style. It is true that in some of her earlier pieces she had rather consciously worked at the inclusion of stylistic devices, but these had never become part of her natural manner of writing and in her later works – perhaps, also, under the pressure of the amount of writing she was called on to do – she had largely given them up. In her autobiography she recounts how a publisher told her, 'You know you have no style,' and although she admits to having been taken aback by such directness she comments, 'Yes, alas! I knew it only too well, and I wished that more time had been left me in which to develop a style'. But time had already done its work, in failing to sow the seeds of a style within her when she was young. Instead, the seeds of other lessons had been sown, and it is doubtful whether she could ever have uprooted the plants which these had become, the plants of honesty, uprightness, directness and simplicity.

Such undeviating virtues, however, she could temper with her own natural characteristics: with a gentle wit, humour, sympathy and understanding, as well as with a clear intelligence, and these were the characteristics which were to stamp her writings and endear her to such a wide readership. But her unvarnished prose is often very readable – at its best, perhaps, when she is expressing her own thoughts, as in the short, pithy articles which she contributed to *The Christian World* for some years under the heading 'Echoes from the Valley', or as in the autobiography, rather than when she is contriving dialogue or drawing out morals for the young.

Marianne Farningham's main work under the name of Eva Hope comprised the biographies of Grace Darling, Queen Victoria,* David Livingstone,* General Gordon,* 'Queens of Literature'* (covering among others Harriet Martineau, Charlotte Brontë and Elizabeth Barrett Browning) and Abraham Lincoln and James Garfield, who are dealt with in one book under the title *New World Heroes*. One cannot say that she was ideally suited to this task, since, apart from other considerations – one of which being that she somewhat relentlessly pushes her subjects into a Christian mould of her own fashioning – her intellectual training was inadequate to fit her for the slow sifting of the facts which go to build up a biography. Nevertheless, it should be borne in mind that this was commissioned work, offered by a publisher who, in the manner of the day, presented it to her as little more than journeyman work, the need to 'select facts and describe them in my own language'. She was promised 'plenty of material' on which to work, and there seems no reason not to blame Mr McAllum of Adam & Co more than Eva Hope for the chapters on 'Ancient Northumbria', 'Lighthouse Homes' and 'The Perils of the Ocean', which go to pad out the 300-plus pages of *Grace Darling*. However, it cannot be denied that the book was to the

---

* I have been unable to track down copies of these works.

taste of the times for enjoyment and instruction intertwined, and it sold well and remains, perhaps, the easiest of Eva Hope's biographies to track down today, in library or second-hand bookshop.

Some years later the firm of Walter Scott was to request Eva Hope to provide a 'Prefatory Notice, Biographical and Critical' to three of the volumes of selections from well known poets which they were bringing out under the series title of 'The Canterbury Poets'. This task, in company with such writers as John Addington Symonds, Ernest Rhys and Mathilde Blind, she performed for Longfellow (1884), Whittier (1885) and Cowper (also 1885). It has to be admitted that Eva Hope's Notices are to be relied on more for their biographical fact – taken from acknowledged sources – than for their critical acumen. Her criticism refers largely to the thought and emotional content. Thus of Whittier: 'He has chosen subjects too sacred to be popular . . . His hymns will be the songs of the Christian church as long as the church remains', and, sadly unprophetically: 'His poems will make it impossible for tyrants to live and prosper'; of Longfellow, replying to criticism that a simpler rhythm would have been more suitable for 'Evangeline': 'Today the poem has become so written in the hearts of the people, that we doubt if one could wish that it had been different in rhythm or any other respect than that which it is'.

Marianne Farningham's writings for children would today be considered to make few concessions to our views of their limited understanding or vocabulary, but we should remember that they were written by someone who could herself read any chapter of the Bible by the time she was six ('so long,' she used to add with a chuckle, 'as she was allowed to skip some of the ugly words!'). In point of fact only a few collections of her writings for the very young were made. *Chats by the Sea*, published in a small, slim volume in 1868, features an omniscient Uncle John who 'loved to teach as well as amuse', and his nephews and niece, Harry, George and Nell, and exemplifies for us in print the mid-nineteenth century teacher. *Little Tales for Little Readers*, which came out in 1869, is a collection of homilies rather than stories, short talks with a practical Christian application. The preface to this collection, in the form of a letter to the children, sets the tone of the small book, combining the light-hearted and the moral in a way which is perhaps peculiarly Victorian:

Dear Little Readers,

. . . Many of you, I suppose, will receive this book as a Christmas-box, or a New Year's gift, or a Birthday present. I wish you a merry Christmas, and a happy New Year, and many happy returns of the day. I hope you will enjoy yourselves very much, that the friends you love the best will be invited to tea, that you may have some new toys, and a Christmas tree, and as many nice things as are good for you.

The moral is reserved for the end of the letter, although the moralist here is already, as she describes herself in her autobiography, 'half a socialist':

> I think, if God spares you, that you will live in very good times, and that you will help to make them better. I am so glad to think that even you whose parents are not rich will be able to go to school,* and learn to read, and write, and think, and that you will not be obliged to work hard and long before you are really old enough, and strong enough; and so I hope you will grow up to be earnest, thoughtful, honourable men and women. And I am just as glad to think that you who will be better off, and not have to work hard at all, will understand that to live well, and do good, and to be even richer in love than in money, is a far surer way to be happy than to live selfishly and sinfully.

In spite of the title of *Little Tales for Little Readers*, one cannot feel that Marianne Farningham is speaking to the *very* young, and in fact one of her most successful works for young people was a volume of advice to older girls, called *Girlhood*. This was a very popular work, first published in 1869, which by 1895, with a new and revised edition, had reached its 25th thousand. Undoubtedly a work which mothers bought for their daughters, there is evidence that daughters, mothers in their turn, valued its counsels enough to buy it for their own daughters. Its 27 short chapters (later expanded to 30) deal with love, with friendship, with leisure and careers, with girls as teachers and girls as servants, with happiness and generosity and health, with fresh air and self-respect. One chapter is devoted to 'Submission', where there is some scorn for what, in the 1895 edition, are described as 'these days of what is foolishly called "the emancipation of women"' – a position which Marianne Farningham takes up more than once in her writing, but which is not really borne out by her own life of independent action. The whole aim of the book (or rather, of this series of papers, since this, like almost all her books, was first serialised in one of the weekly papers for which she wrote) was to train girls to be sweet, true and gentle, which the author saw as the epitome of the good Englishwoman – and a precondition of which was being a good (and happy!) Christian.

The success of *Girlhood* was followed up by a series on *Boyhood*, published the following year, and containing chats on such subjects as manliness, courage, good-natured boys, perseverance, conquerors, growing boys, 'What shall I be?', bunglers, and fun. Books of advice represent a genre which has almost completely died out today, although the tradition is perhaps continued, in a less moralising way, by a few agony columns in popular

---

* The Education Act of 1870 would ensure the provision of schooling for all children.

magazines. In 1870, however, Messrs James Clarke & Co, as representatives of the media of the day, clearly had their finger on the pulse of the times when they published these collections.

There were also longer stories for children, such as *Brothers and Sisters*, the tale of a Christian family growing up, but most of Marianne Farningham's stories (all originally serialised in either *The Christian World* or *The Sunday School Times*) seem to be aimed at a slightly older audience – what we today would call teenage readers. Such, for example, are two stories which were reprinted as paperbacks in the 1870s by James Clarke and Hodder & Stoughton, *What of the Night?* and *Dell's New Year*. The first of these is a temperance tale, which daringly and vividly portrays an alcoholic pastor. The second could perhaps be described as a Christian romance, in which a girl 'who has everything' moves from nihilism (and the unwanted attentions of her guardian's son, Ethelbert) to Christianity and a recognition of the worth of a penniless teacher of arithmetic and shorthand. Marianne Farningham's later stories frequently make use of romance as a secondary theme, often combined with a dark mystery which has to be solved before true love can run its course – a device which she may have learnt from the work of Emma Jane Worboise, a popular novelist of some talent who also wrote for *The Christian World*.

Some of Marianne Farningham's most interesting work dates from the 1890s and early 1900s, and among this are two full-length stories which she serialised in *The Sunday School Times*. One of these was *A Window in Paris*, which was based on the recollections of a family who had lived through the days of the Franco-Prussian war in Paris in 1870. This is sometimes described as a novel, but is in fact largely reportage, at second hand, of scenes that actually occurred, interwoven with a not wholly convincing romance. It was written from the best of motives, the furtherance of peace, but a tale of siege, deprivation and death requires above all a fitting language, and Marianne Farningham's domestic vocabulary is simply not strong enough to carry it. It is true that under terrible conditions the mere fact of continuing existence obliges people to perform, as best they can, the usual humdrum actions of everyday life. Nevertheless, she is incapable of representing the overhanging threat or the horror in which this must ultimately crystallise. While she is to be congratulated on tackling a subject which did not consort well with Victorian cosiness she could not rid herself of the trappings of this.

There is, however, a further difficulty inherent in her plea for pacifism. Having bound herself to a theory of the submission of women to men she could not, as a woman, urge her views as superior to those of men if and when they elected to go to war. She could then only fall back on patriotism, a word whose very etymology ironically underlines the pre-eminence of the male.

Of considerably greater interest is *Nineteen Hundred? A Forecast and a Story*, which appeared in 1892. Here, if anywhere, we have the quintessential Marianne Farningham of the prose writings. While the 32 chapters do indeed tell a tale and make a forecast which is not without interest, the various elements of which the story is composed prove, on inspection, to be mainly events from Marianne Farningham's own life; the people too perhaps, if one knew them better, taken from her own immediate circle. Certainly she has written herself into the story, as Miss Wentworth, the elderly but capable teacher, who helps in the running of girls' classes and clubs.

The main setting of the story is none other than her early home in Kent, the village of Farningham, lightly disguised as Darentdale, while the site chosen for a new settlement in the country for Arthur Knight's London factory workers is Craighelbyl, named after her own Barmouth cottage, Craig-yr-Helbul. Not only do we have the sudden illumination of authentic scenes from Farningham, such as:

> The village post-office closed early; and the postman had just called, in his curious red cart, drawn by a gaunt horse that was celebrated for getting over the ground quickly, and having received the bag, was hastening away to the nearest town,

but events which occurred in the neighbourhood are also reconstituted to suit the new story: the 'Happy Exodus' of Arthur Knight's workers to Craighelbyl, for example, echoes the triumphant installation of the occupants of the Farningham Homes for Little Boys in the hills above Horton Kirby in 1866. The name of one of the three heroines, Thomasine Grace (Tom for short), commemorates both Grace Darling and her sister Thomasin, to whom the biography had been dedicated. The educated, sensitive Mary Wythburn, who becomes for a time 'the Basket Woman', is perhaps someone the writer must have known well from her Bristol days, Anna Waring, the hymn-writer, who once, taking over her basket from a flower-seller who had for a while more pressing business to see to, sold violets in the street.

But when all the correspondences and identifications have been made, and the resulting well crafted patchwork is spread out and examined on all sides, we are left to consider the frame, the background which brings all the pieces together. In the pages of this writer there can be no question of the accuracy and the sincerity with which she describes the problem which all her characters are addressing: the misery and the destitution which were to be found in the lowest levels of society at this time. England was riding to unrivalled prosperity, and yet very little was being done to ensure that everyone partook of the wealth to which nearly everyone contributed. The poverty and starvation which made Mary Wythburn 'get(s) into a furious mood when she sees hosts of poor wretches starving because they cannot get remunerative work to do', are not things which we immediately associate with millions in the years around Queen Victoria's jubilee. Arthur Knight levels at greed, cruelty, lust, drunkenness, slavery, hypocrisy, fraud. The earnestness preached by the writer of *Little Tales for Little Readers*, in 1869, was an earnestness which she herself felt and was prepared, over twenty years later, to try to put into practice, by encouraging her own circles to 'lead the way'.

In her autobiography Marianne Farningham owns to intense disappointment that the social improvements which she foretold did not come to pass, 'for my hopes were, and still are, that some time during the century, though possibly late, and gradually, the character of English life may be raised to the high estate which I tried to describe'. If, for a few decades during the twentieth century, the aim and frequently the reality was adequate housing, an enriching education, and time and money for leisure pursuits, we should recognise in this connection the driving force of those many Victorians, Marianne Farningham among them, who felt that it was no longer enough that 'the higher pleasures and pursuits' should remain 'the exclusive privileges of the favoured few'. Marianne Farningham is particularly remarkable among such voices as a woman who rose from the working class to join the fight for a general improvement in the English citizen's lot. *Nineteen Hundred?* is full of practical suggestions, still worthy of consideration – for dealing with strikes, for home ownership, for stamping out drunkenness, for example. It is the work of a woman of wit, wisdom and common sense, who felt that the obvious and practical way of dealing with a problem was the only way, which should not be shirked for the sake of political or selfish considerations.

The autobiography, *A Working Woman's Life*, published in 1907, also falls into the category of Marianne Farningham's prose writings, but is naturally of a somewhat different kind. Although she was used to communicating with others, particularly on the basis of shared experience, she clearly did not find it easy, towards the end of her life, to lay that life bare, akin to exposing the well-spring of one's creative self for all to see. What we are given (apart from the first few chapters, reproduced here) is the public person, rather than the private one; the title, *A Working Woman's Life*, is well chosen.

The childhood recollections are sincere, full, artless. I suspect that these chapters were written quite quickly and had, in a sense, been waiting to be written for many years. The fifteen later chapters, on the other hand, are somewhat drier – not because Marianne Farningham is less open, but because out of so long a working life, packed with events and above all with people, it must have been difficult to decide what to put in and what to leave out. The autobiographer, unlike the biographer, has too much material. As it is, there is due homage – to friends, to colleagues in church and press, to those she moved among – spiced with much that is lively: touches of humour and, as in her lectures, tales that 'told against' herself, as well as tributes received from members of her Bible Class and others. Finally, she is reluctant to close: her last three chapters are entitled 'Relinquishments', 'Aftermath' and 'Eventide'. But, when the time comes, like the devout Christian and good public speaker that she was, she can find suitable words of benediction with which to leave her reader, gazing at the barely-seen faces of her girls' Bible Class in the twilight, as they close one of their meetings singing an evening hymn from Anna Waring's *Hymns and Meditations* – the same one that, dying, she would ask her niece to read aloud to her.

Marianne Farningham was always a writer who spoke directly from and about her faith, and it is undoubtedly true to say that all her life this was the most important thing to her. Jonathan Whittemore had invited her, early on, to write hymns herself, but she never attained to any considerable eminence as a hymn-writer, although some of her hymns were included in Sankey's and other popular collections. The freer forms of a less fettered poetry and of journalism were more suited to her style and her thought. Most of this, however, written as it was for either *The Christian World* or *The Sunday School Times*, espoused and reinforced the religious message of those papers. She wrote several series of devotional papers, or homilies, and also did a considerable amount of Biblical exegesis: for many years in *The Sunday School Times* she contributed what were known as the 'Bible Readings for Senior Scholars on the International Lesson'; *Sunday Afternoons with Jesus*, sub-titled *Bible readings on the life of Christ*, which came out in 1874, was based on lessons which she had herself given to her girls' class.

Much as she loved the young (and as they loved her: she once showed a friend part of a letter beginning 'Dear little mother', which had been dropped into her hand as she waved goodbye to a party of girls who had been holidaying with her at Barmouth), as she grew older she found herself writing for the old, out of her own experience. *In Evening Lights*, of 1897, is a collection of short religious papers, each based on a text, written with her usual penetration and common-sense. This is a deeply felt work, facing up to such things as personal loss and also, a subject not often tackled, the loss of oneself as death approaches. Care, even love, for those she is addressing illuminate the pages of this short book.

An advertisement of 1869 for *The Christian World* describes it as 'perfectly unsectarian', and as representing 'all Evangelical Denominations'. Marianne Farningham, on the whole, shared her paper's broad outlook, although she underwent some misery when, later, it was castigated as being too broad by one of her own denomination, the Baptist preacher Charles Haddon

Spurgeon who had written frequently for *The Christian World* in its early days. The nineteenth century was one of strongly held religious beliefs, beliefs which could, however, be influenced by each other. In Marianne Farningham's first collection of poems, *Lays and Lyrics of the Blessed Life*, we can detect the influence of John Keble and, through him, of the high-church Oxford Movement, on a dissenting mind.

This is particularly noticeable in the first and longest poem 'Light from the Cross' which develops an idea taken from Keble. In spite of this, however, the poem flings its appeal wide, preaching a Christianity that will illuminate peoples and countries, art and science, ecumenism and social philanthropy. There is even a visionary strain in the poem:

> I hear the indistinct, slow future's tramp
> Marching along the beaten way of time;
> In its broad hands it bears the gospel lamp,
> And on its lofty brow God's seal sublime!

But this was not to remain a permanent feature of her writing, for with her natural preference for 'doing the next thing' she would concentrate on trying to improve the shining hour rather than the era.

Although most of the poems in *Lays and Lyrics* are devotional, there are again traces of the nature poet, who would come more to the fore in the later collections. Many poems, too, display a youthful joy and optimism, and while the youthful joy was of necessity transmuted, a sunny optimism, although submerged for some years, is a strong characteristic of Marianne Farningham's later work.

With the title poem of her second collection, *Gilbert and other Poems* (as also with her novel, *The Cathedral's Shadow*) she was to atone for the backsliding of a dissenter with a severe attack on the 'Romanist' church, attacking in particular the curtailment of freedom which she saw as following on adherence to Rome. She was not alone in her century in being thus troubled by the allurements of the Roman Catholic church: reaction to Catholic Emancipation was strong from many quarters.

Both *Gilbert*, of 1866, and *Leaves from Elim*, her third collection, of 1873, are considerably darker in tone than the earlier work, and more metaphysical: images from nature are more likely to have a metaphorical content than to be brought in for their own sake. Thus, as in 'Across the Sea', from *Leaves from Elim*:

> To the sloping bank where the waves are creeping –
> The waves that me from my home divide, –
> I come and look in the time of weeping
> To the lighted shore on the other side,

nature is subservient to Christian theology, and the poems feature thoughts of the hereafter rather than the here. Nevertheless, at the time these poems were being written Marianne Farningham was specifically rejecting the image of 'the gloomy Christian', and we should beware of attributing the more sombre tones of *Gilbert* and *Leaves from Elim* to her religion. The fourth verse of 'A Time to Sing', from *Leaves from Elim*, for example, although borrowing an image from Christianity, carries no specific Christian message in the following lines:

> The winter locked me in a narrow tomb,
> And the unbroken silence kept me down;
> I could not sing for all the pain and gloom,
> And the sharp pressure of the thorn-girt crown;
> I did not even dream of liberty,
> Or hope that joy would ever come to me.

It is important to remember how frequently Victorians were brought face to face with the obverse of life, death – and not with the merciful swiftness of an accident, although there were those, too, on roads, railways and in factories, but through the more lingering course of an illness, particularly consumption. The less well off one was, the greater were bound to be one's losses, in relatives and friends. It is also quite possible that this was a time for Marianne Farningham herself of personal checks and disappointments. Whatever the reason for the darkness of this period in her life, she saw her religion throughout as offering a beacon in the night, a 'lighted shore' in the distance.

Significantly, she emerges from this period of melancholy with a collection of poems entitled *Songs of Sunshine*. In these poems she specifically rejects her earlier espoused view of the world as a vale of tears. The delightfully titled 'Time of the Singing of Birds', for example, ends,

> Let the sadness and the sorrow
>   For God's brighter gifts make room,
> Since the time of the glad singing
>   Of the merry birds has come;
> Let us also sing sweet praises,
>   God has caused the spring to be!
> There's a part in earth's full chorus,
>   Friend, for you and me.

This is also the voice of the Marianne Farningham of the later collections, *Harvest Gleanings* (1903) and *Lyrics of the Soul* (1908), the Marianne Farningham who, although her autobiography is very discreet, clearly fell in love more than once. While she continued to write many purely devotional poems, only in her middle and later years was she at last able to let the outflow of her own personal feelings, for friends and lovers, rise unconstrainedly and mingle with her love of nature and her love of Christ. Many of her best poems are those of someone fulfilled by love and able to recognise it as the greatest good: the sun which opens the flower, the source of all beauty, all benefits. It is this fusing of the three most passionate strains in her life which gives us the lyrical sweetness of some of the poems printed in the Appendix, taken from *Harvest Gleanings* and *Lyrics of the Soul.*

Certain weaknesses have to be admitted, in particular a somewhat restricted choice of words and occasional triteness. Such defects, however, are directly traceable to the writer's early life and to the constraints which journalism put upon her. On the one hand, the paucity of her education and the narrowness of her upbringing left her with a permanently limited vocabulary; on the other, the demands of her trade meant that her weekly poems were dashed off as required – and frequently at the last minute, to be seized by 'a friend who could run' who would catch the post for her – with little or no time left for revision. But these flaws should not obscure for us her real gifts as a poet, nor the many very lovely lines which were the outcome of her simplicity of style. On the evidence of her poetry alone, if on no other, Marianne Farningham was a woman whose working life merits better than oblivion.

PART II

from A Working Woman's Life

Marianne Farningham in her late 60s, at the time when she was engaged on her autobiography.
From the frontispiece to *Harvest Gleanings*.

Chapter One

A CHILD OF THE COUNTRY

I begin the story of my life on a March day in the first year of the new century. The air is full of retrospect. The passing of the nineteenth century, and the death of the great and beloved Queen, have forced back the thoughts of the people, and for a little while, before the flood of the new times carries us onward, we all halt for a moment or two and think of the past. I have a past to think of, too, and though there is nothing very remarkable to make it worth the telling, every life is interesting, and perhaps I may have a few friends in different parts of the country who will care to read the simple story of a worker's life. So, while the birds are singing the old love song in a new spring, the primroses are opening their eyes in the woods, and the trees are covered with buds pushing their way to the light, I will try to forget how far I am on into the autumn, and go back to the sweet fair days of my spring.

I had the good fortune to be born in the country. Farningham is a winsome little village on the banks of the Darent, in the midst of the garden of Kent, and halfway between London and the county town. It was on 17 December 1834 that I came into the world, the first child of my parents, who were married on the previous Christmas Day. My father, Joseph Hearn, was a small tradesman, and my mother, whose maiden name was Rebecca Bowers, was the daughter of a working paper-maker, who was also a preacher of great force and originality. My earliest recollections are of a wonder why, whenever he preached, the chapel seemed always full, and why people both laughed and cried during his discourse.

I can recall my grandfather, Mr George Bowers, of Eynsford, as I saw him on several occasions. In the pulpit I always thought he looked a very fine man. Seated in our kitchen, talking with some old friend, each smoking a long clay pipe, and with a glass of home-brewed beer on the table, as was customary then, I was a little afraid of the keen eyes that watched me. He and his friends spoke on high themes, of Calvinistic doctrine and the heresies of Arminianism, and sometimes they lapsed into village gossip. I always tried to understand, and was always bewildered. I remember him, too, as the host of his family on Christmas Day. He had a large number of sons and daughters – I think about a dozen – and most of them had large families too, but we all kept Christmas together in the old house 'down the lane' until we were quite too many even for that hospitable table. His wife, my grandmother Bowers, was a sweet, placid old lady, and some of the proudest moments of my life were when she took my arm as we walked to chapel together. She must have been very short, for I was not then full-grown – indeed, I never have been – and she died when I was about eighteen.* My grandfather lived to be a very old man, and as long as he was able he walked many miles to the different villages to preach. He kept his keen wit and spirituality to the end. A friend once told me that he said to him, 'Creasy, I shall die in debt.' 'How is that?' asked Mr Creasy. 'Why, I can never pay the thanks I owe, for gratitude can't keep pace with mercies,' he replied.

My father's mother lived with us, a dear old lady, who thought beautiful thoughts, and expressed them in beautiful language. She wrote poetry, and her prayers always seemed to take me into heaven. It was she who taught me to read, and, strange as it seems now, I was thought to be rather a prodigy because when I was six years old I could read any chapter in the Bible. The Bible, indeed, was my only lesson-book then and for years after. How I loved it! In it I found an inheritance of wealth which has made me rich all my life. My grandmother also taught me a prayer, written by Isaac Watts, in monosyllables –

> May I live to know and fear Thee,
>   Trust and love Thee all my days,
> Then go dwell for ever near Thee,
>   See thy face, and sing Thy praise.

The last thing I remember of my grandmother Hearn was one night during a terrible thunderstorm. I think there have never been such thunderstorms as those we had at Farningham. She was ill and in bed, and we were all in her room. I recall how peaceful she was through the storm, and that it quieted my fear to hold her hand. She was very deaf. There was an awful clap of thunder that seemed as if it would bring the house down. She opened her eyes with a smile, and asked, 'Was that thunder?' And then she repeated a verse which we do not often hear now –

> This awful God is ours,
>   Our Father and our Friend,
> He will send down His heavenly powers,
>   To keep us to the end.

---

* Altered from 'about eight' in the original, clearly a misprint or an oversight.

My father and mother were both members of the Baptist church at Eynsford, a pretty village about a mile from Farningham. They were both Sunday school teachers; indeed, the life of the chapel was their life, and it became mine. I have been told that when I was a month old, and my mother was able for the first time to go to chapel, she took the baby too. It was customary to have tea in the vestry. After tea the friends went into the chapel, and I was laid, happily asleep, on the table in what was known as the 'singing pew,' in which at the ordinary services the choir sat. As those who formed the tea-party were interested in the new baby which had come to Joseph and Rebecca, they held a prayer-meeting for the child. I have always had the feeling that no baptismal service in any church, though performed by a priest, assisted by godfathers and godmothers, could have been a more real consecration than that simple prayer-meeting in the village chapel. I was a 'child of many prayers,' and delight to think friends prayed for me when for the first time I entered a chapel.

The influence of this little dissenting church and its associations, not only on my own early life, but on that of our neighbours, was very great. Eynsford, through its agency, touched many other villages. It was a 'Particular Baptist Church,' founded in 1775, and consisted at its formation of five members, who were baptised in the Darent on a profession of their faith in the Lord Jesus. Its first meeting-house was a stable fitted up for the purpose. Much opposition and persecution attended its inception, but the little cause grew and flourished in spite of that. In 1802 a young Baptist minister became its pastor, whose name, John Rogers, will be revered through all generations, for he was one of the most distinguished of the Nonconformist ministers of the time, a man of remarkable ability, of noble character and great power and influence, richly endowed by the Spirit of God. Two years later a new chapel was erected, which for a hundred years was the home of devotion and love. The wife of Mr Rogers was the sister of my Grandmother Hearn; they were both strong, sweet women, of considerable culture and striking mental powers, both women of unflinching principles and strong convictions. I have said that my grandmother was deaf, but she always attended the services, and Mr Rogers said she was his great helper, for while he preached she prayed, 'Save Thy people. Bless Thine inheritance.' The church was absolutely Calvinistic, as well as Particular Baptist. Other churches were judged to be in error; but Mrs Rogers wanted to tell the people that every one who would might be saved. It is curious to-day to remember what fierce fights were once fought under the two banners of Calvinism and Free Will. I am ashamed to say that the only recollection I have personally of Mr Rogers is that of his giving me some plums, pushed through his garden gate one at a time.

I love to think of my child-life in those two villages, Farningham and Eynsford. My father, who never had a yard of land of his own, had a passion for building, and in our little garden he erected two outhouses. One was a workshop, and the other was for domestic purposes – a place in which the washing could be done, and with a loft above for storage. This loft was a place of mystery to me. There were several hives of bees, and there were openings through the walls for their convenience, and my father took as much pains with their homes as with his own. He made models of various places of interest. Among the rest was Windsor Castle, a duplicate of which he made and sent to the Prince Consort, who returned him an autograph letter of thanks. My father was very fond of his bees, and he and they were good friends. I remember once he took me up with him to perform a curious little ceremony. He had lost a cousin, and he told me he was going to inform the bees, and they would say they were sorry. He tapped the hive, and then said in a low, quiet voice, 'My cousin is dead,' and I felt a cold shiver pass over me, as I distinctly heard a wailing response like a buzzing moan from the bees. There was also in the loft a telescope, through which I often looked into the heart of a beautiful wood that was a mile or two away.

My father intended to use the lower part of this building as a small private brewery, and he had just secured all the necessary utensils for brewing his own beer, when some great temperance orator, perhaps Father Mathew, came to the village. My father was convinced, and became one of the first total abstainers. The next day he told me about it, and, showing me the pledge which he had signed, asked me if I would like my name to go down with his. I could not write, so he guided my hand, and together we wrote my name. It was rather hard in those days to be a teetotaller, and at the parties to which I was invited I had to endure much. My father had just been made a deacon, and a lady told him that if she had known he was going to be an abstainer she would not have voted for him, as his conduct was most unscriptural!

In course of time other children came to keep me company, until there were five of us, three girls and two boys. We went to Sunday school as soon as we were able to walk the distance, the girls always being dressed exactly alike. There was no day school to which we could go. A young ladies' boarding establishment existed, to which, quite early in my life, I turned longing eyes, but the charges were too high for my father's means. There was also the National school connected with the Church of England, but we were never allowed to go there. It was then, as now, a Nonconformist principle not to allow Chapel children to learn the Church Catechism, and whatever might have been my father's opinion, his fellow-members considered it a far greater sin to send children to the National school than to let them remain uneducated. At Eynsford there was a small dame school, to which I went for a little while, but for the most part all our early lessons came from our parents, chiefly, of course, our mother. She taught us to sweep and clean, sew and knit, to mend and make, and to be careful in the exercise of all household arts. 'Think of what you are doing,' was a frequent hint given to me, because, when I was darning stockings, or sewing seams, or even dusting a room, my thoughts were generally 'over the hills and far away,' for I began to dream as soon as I began to think. It was a beautiful world of fancy in which I lived, and I saw lovely sights, and did heroic deeds; and my everyday life was beautiful too, for it was filled with love, the joy of doing, and much running about in the open air.

I had the one great illness of my life when I was very young indeed. I can just remember the hours of delirium and suffering. It was small-pox with complications. Once I seemed to come out of the confusion of my brain, and saw mother wringing her hands with tears running down her cheeks, and I heard her say, 'My poor little dying child; O Lord, take care of her.' I do not remember refusing to let our minister pray with me, but my mother afterwards told me that I did, to her very great grief and anxiety, for it filled her with fear in regard to my spiritual state. She was not quite comforted until months after, when the prizes were given in the Sunday school, and I chose for mine a volume of *Sermons to Children*, though I have not the remotest idea why.

It was a long and weary period of convalescence through which I passed, and I lay in utter weakness and prostration day after day. My bed was an old-fashioned four-poster, with white hangings and curtains. They were trimmed with tassels, and these tassels were a constant source of interest to me. I called them men and women, or children, walking in procession, sometimes to a school-treat, but oftener to a funeral, and I used to wonder if it were my own. The next thing I remember was a terrible hunger that would not be appeased. I have seldom felt myself so badly treated since as in those days when roast apples took so long to roast, and my mother turned deaf ears to my entreaties for cake, and ruthlessly cut away all the fat from my specially cooked mutton chop. But I remember how sweetly and tenderly she seemed to love me in those days, and how there was a strange difference in the way in which she talked to me.

We had a beautiful old family Bible with pictures, and this was always brought out on Sunday evenings, and we used to sit and stand around our mother while she told us stories. It seemed that every Sunday evening, before bedtime, we went to Bethlehem. Every little touch and incident was so dwelt upon that the Holy Birth became part of our life. All the words of Jesus grew so familiar to us that we were never able to forget them after. We were taught to repeat them reverently long before we could understand them, and they have never seemed more beautiful than in those first days. But we had our Old Testament favourites too; Baby Moses was always 'a dear little thing,' and Joseph in the pit, and Daniel in the lions' den, were tragedies which, when we were away by ourselves, we often acted. The Bible was in our home the children's library. We were never told fairytales, but our mother used often to recite to us Jane Taylor's 'Moral Songs,' and we had our share of old nursery rhymes, and dearly loved 'Old Mother Hubbard' and 'Little Red Riding-Hood,' though I am not quite sure that they held their own with Jonah and the whale.

My first attempt at rhyming was an epitaph on a dead toad which we found in the garden, and which we put in a match-box and buried with great solemnity. I could not write the epitaph, for in the matter of writing I was quite behind the other children of my age. My ignorance in this respect was a sore trouble to me, and I made the lives of my parents a burden to them with my continual cry' 'Teach me to write.' At length a very pleasant plan was thought of. The next house but one to ours was the home of the Reverend John Rogers; his youngest daughter, Isabella, hearing of my childish desire, kindly undertook to teach me to write. My father took great pains with a little box in the shape of a book, which he made to hold my copy-book, pen, ink, ruler, and pencil, and which I proudly carried under my arm when I went to receive my writing-lesson.

Two incidents illustrate the awakening of the soul of a child. Seated on a footstool, I was one morning rocking my brother in his cradle, with a bound volume of *The Sailor's Magazine* in my lap. Some of our ancestors were seafaring folk, and I have an indistinct idea that one of them was the Captain Gibbon, who first brought mahogany into England. I think it was my Grandmother Hearn who gave me the magazine to read while I rocked baby. Turning over the leaves, I found two poems, which had a marvellous effect upon me. One was about a family Bible, and the last line of each stanza was –

The old-fashioned Bible that lay on the stand.

The other was the hand of an angel that led me into a wonderful world of vivid imagination and unutterable joy. It was 'The Better Land,' by Felicia Hemans. I wish I could describe, even if only so far as I am able to live it again, the strange, sweet emotions which overcame me as I read those lines. I remember that having read through the poem, I was obliged, to prevent myself from being overcome by faintness, to put down the book and go to the door for a breath of fresh air, though the baby had not gone to sleep and soon summoned me back to duty by loud cries. How the music and the rhythm charmed me! Quite what I saw I cannot remember, as I repeated softly to myself –

> Is it far away in some region old,
> Where rivers wander o'er sands of gold,
> Where the burning rays of the ruby shine,
> And the diamond lights up the secret mine,
> And the pearl gleams forth from the coral strand:
> Is it there, sweet mother, this better land?

It was at this time that Nature claimed me and drew me to her very heart. At the bottom of our garden, and past the two buildings, was a wall, just low enough for me to look over, and also to get over on many happy holidays. I must have spent hours, as a child, leaning against that wall and looking out into the world of summer. First there was a meadow, and a gate out of it led into another meadow, in which was a row of magnificent lime-trees, which I loved and almost worshipped – even now the scent of the limes can make me feel a child again. At the end of this meadow was the river Darent, which made music day and night; in it watercress grew, and such forget-me-nots as are not to be found in the world beside, and over it the willows bent, and God's skies of blessing stretched. Then far away in the blue distances were gentle hills, and shady woods, and picturesque little villages. This view from our garden wall was never the same two days together. I could always find surprise of loveliness hidden away in some corner of it. It was ever beautiful, spring, summer, autumn, or winter. The summer sunsets were heavenly; indeed, it often seemed to me that heaven itself was just over there as far as my eye could reach, and I have many a time imagined groups of angels and the 'innumerable company' moving about in the masses of white and golden clouds. Often I have stood with tears in my eyes, and my heart throbbing with love and gladness, and tried to say something to God to let Him know what I was feeling. I wonder if He took the child's silent ecstasy for praise!

I was never allowed to stay long enough to satisfy me, for the cheery voice of my mother would call me into the house to amuse my brothers and sisters, or do some work. I am afraid she was grieved at my evident love of standing still and gazing. On one or two occasions, to my utter shame, she broke in upon me when I was talking to myself, and ordered me to sweep the carpet all over again, or showed me some article of furniture which I ought to have dusted. Dear mother! she did not like my always having a book in my hand or pocket, and would have been better pleased if I had been equally fond of the brush or the needle; but she did her best to keep me at work all day, only letting me have books and magazines when my tasks were done. She took care, however, to give us all a very good time. She loved to see us play and to play with us. She was so proud to see us looking pretty and clean that we were always sorry when we had spoiled her handiwork, though I am afraid my repentance had not much practical effect, for I was a rollicking, mischievous child, often getting into trouble.

Once, in trying to get through a hedge, I tore a pinafore that was nearly new. A poor, sobered, remorseful child I was as I went home, with the thought of my mother before me. It happened, however, that she was out, and so I put myself to bed that night. Kneeling beside the bed, and repeating my prayers, the thought of God suddenly came to me. In a flash I remembered what I had been told about Him, that He was good and great and could do everything, that He loved good children, and even forgave naughty ones; and the thought occurred to me that I had only to pray and He would mend my pinafore for me. So I asked Him to do it, saying over and over again, 'O Lord, have mercy upon me, and mend my pinafore for me, for Jesus Christ's sake, Amen.' Then I got into bed and waited, closing my eyes in awe and expectation. Several times I got out to pray again and examine the hole, and at first it seemed to me that it was really getting smaller, but after a time the disappointing conviction was forced upon me that the hole remained exactly the same; and I lay in my bed softly sobbing for the unanswered prayer – not knowing how many thousands had done so before me. I had several aunts whom I loved, sisters of my mother, but the dearest was Aunt Mary. She came into the room, and, stooping to kiss me, discovered that I was awake and crying. I was comforted and quieted in her kind arms, and soon told her the whole story – how anxious I was that mother should not know that I had torn my pinafore, and how disappointed I was in God. Said my aunt, 'I will mend it for you. Perhaps that is God's way of answering you. Perhaps He sent me here to-night on purpose. Now try to trust in Him and go to sleep.' I did; and never a word did I hear from my mother about that torn pinafore. I have many times since imagined the smiles of the little family group downstairs, but I think it was very sweet of them not to laugh away my faith.

Chapter Two

CHILDHOOD

My first real sorrow was the death of my little brother, the eldest son, but that memory is so faint that I think my parents must have deliberately resolved not to let it overshadow us more than was necessary. I remember seeing my father walk about with him in his arms, and that we were told afterwards how the Good Shepherd had taken our little brother Alfred to be with Him. Also I remember that we were all put into black frocks and white diaper pinafores, and that we wore white socks and patent strap-shoes.

On the night of the funeral I could not sleep, and I lay listening to the nightingales. Our house was nearly opposite the vicarage garden, or at least it was near enough for the sounds to come to me through the stillness of the night. The birds thrilled and comforted me strangely. At first I was half frightened, thinking the singers must be something more than birds, the sounds were so loud as well as sweet; but afterwards I remembered what I had heard about nightingales, and was sure the songs were theirs. The nightingales in the vicarage garden were delightful realities to me in all the summers of my childhood's life, for there were many nights when I was sweetly disturbed by their singing, and I linked them with heaven.

I must have been between nine and ten when there was a grand achievement by the Nonconformists of our villages, and I had my heart's desire, and went to school! Joseph Lancaster and his schools were so talked about that even Farningham and Eynsford heard of them. The necessity of educating the children was felt more and more, and two or three men had consciences that would not let them rest because of the wrongs and losses of the little ones of the chapels; and therefore, under the auspices of the British and Foreign School Society, a building was erected at Eynsford. On the day of the opening of the school my mother took me and my next sister, Rebecca, and we were among the first scholars enrolled. It was a great event, an almost unprecedented thing for our mother to be out in the morning with her children. My youngest sister, Hephzibah, was also with us, but the authorities decided that Heppie was too young to be admitted, much to that little person's wrath and disappointment.

All the Farningham scholars took their dinners to school, and we had glorious times in that dinner-hour. The river ran at the bottom of a short meadow near the playground, and was a source of endless interest to us. Curious scenes were enacted on the bank, and many dangerous games were played. One of the willows was bent over the water, stretching half across the stream, and of course that was our favourite tree. I often conducted a baptismal service there! As my friends were Baptists, it goes without saying that it was a baptism by immersion. We dressed up all sorts of things in the school towels. I stood upon the extreme edge of the trunk, and the boys on the bank, who represented the deacons, passed the candidates on to me, and with more or less difficulty I dipped them, while the other children on the bank sang Hallelujah. The ceremony was the most easily accomplished when the river was full, for it was impossible to maintain a ministerial dignity when stooping low, or lying flat on the trunk, in order to reach the water. We were found out all too soon, for we had an accident which probably prevented a much greater catastrophe. My sister took off her pinafore to wrap round 'the candidate,' which was that day the school bucket, and they floated away together. We all tried with sticks and umbrellas to get it out, but did not succeed in reaching it. The loss of two such valuable things as the pinafore and the bucket naturally occasioned considerable questioning, and the truth came out, Punishment was meted to the offenders in what we considered quite undue and undeserved measure. There was also an abiding penalty, for we were forbidden ever to go into that meadow again during the dinner-hour.

I was plenteously punished at school for my general naughtiness, and at home for my lack of reverence for the solemn subject of baptism. I was the most sorry because my governess, whom I loved, called me a ringleader. Indeed, I must have been a very naughty little girl, for I remember one teacher telling me, in the Sunday school, that, but for the facts of my being a child of many prayers, and that nothing was too hard for the Lord, she would think there could be no salvation for me, and that I was certain to be sent to hell! I was extremely shocked, and was glad when, soon after, the superintendent put me into another class.

I loved both the day and the Sunday school, being passionately eager to learn, and I really wanted to be good, though I think no one understood this but my mother. I used to be examined at home in regard to what I learned at the British school, and my father often said, 'I do not think you are learning anything whatever there, only they are managing to make you more intelligent,' which was perhaps the best way of educating me.

The knowledge received at the Sunday school was, however, very definite and dogmatic. It was a happy thing, for which I have been thankful all my life, that I was made to learn by heart long passages of Scripture. Let no one think that this was ever a hardship. The grand themes, and the stately, beautiful language in which they were told, fed my very life. I think the first I learned was the twenty-third psalm, and there has never been any time when every sentence has not appealed to me. The fifty-first also was a great favourite – it expressed so much of what I felt. The Gospel of St John I learned from beginning to end, and the heart and mind of the child never saw the slightest difficulty in it. Many chapters in the other Gospels were also committed to memory, and some from the Epistles. Naturally I did not understand them, nor even try to, but I knew that they dealt with high things, and delighted in the words. As to the hymns which I learned, and repeated to my teachers, I am amazed that books containing them were ever put into the hands of children. Of course, like everybody in the school, I learned –

There is a dreadful hell,
   And everlasting pains,
Where sinners must with devils dwell
   In darkness, fire, and chains

We sang the words glibly enough and without much thought of what they meant, but I am none the less sure that the theology of the day, and particularly of those hymns, had considerable influence on the minds of the young singers. Hell was a very real thing to me, and I had a curious fancy, when a very young child, that it was underground, and that there was one entrance to it from a certain place just outside Farningham, which was called Whitepost Hill. Many a time when I have been walking up that road alone, with a weight of many sins upon my conscience, I have been afraid there would be an earthquake, which would swallow me up; and I have run over it in breathless haste and with panting prayers. Once, in a very dry season, there was a slight fissure in the road, and until the merciful rain came and healed it I often slipped away from my home to see if it had grown wider, for I quite expected to meet my doom there.

   Much of the religious teaching of the day was far more sombre than it should have been, and I rejoice to think that only the happier side of Christian life and theology is presented to the children of to-day. The following hymn is one which I learned when very young, and it was one of my chief favourites too, though now I should blame any teacher who allowed a merry child to learn by heart such sentiments in regard to 'the life that is.' We sang what was not true, for the land was not barren, neither was it a vale of tears.

Young as I am, with pilgrim feet,
Father, I travel to Thy seat;
And, leaning on my Saviour's hand,
Prepare to leave this barren land.

My cradle was beset with fears,
My infant eyes o'erflowed with tears,
Ere I could good or evil know,
My little heart was filled with woe.

While o'er this desert world I roam,
Teach me to seek a better home;
Unstained by woe, unchanged by years,
Unlike this gloomy vale of tears.

This hymn was in the little book published by the Sunday School Union, in a red-leather binding, which many of us well remember. Most of the hymns were bright enough, and a special favourite at that time was 'Hosanna,' a hymn written for the Sunday School Jubilee. 'I think when I read that sweet story of old,' and 'See Israel's gentle Shepherd stands' were also very dear to us.

There was another hymn sung in our school once a year, on Whit Sunday, the moral tendency of which was no doubt good, but which brought painful blushes to the cheeks of many of the girls. It was the fashion in Kent to put on our new summer clothes for the first time on that day, when the gallery on which the scholars sat suddenly bloomed into a flower-garden. Our Sunday school treat was always held on Whit Monday, so that altogether it was a gay and festive time. Our good old superintendent, Mr Whitehead, seeing the pretty array of the girls before him, never failed to give out with great emphasis – two lines at a time, because not many of us had books – these verses –

Why should our garments, made to hide
Our parents' shame, provoke our pride?
The art of dress did ne'er begin,
Till Eve, our mother, learned to sin.

When first she put the covering on,
Her robe of innocence was gone!
And yet her children vainly boast
In the sad marks of glory lost.

How proud we are, how fond to show
Our clothes, and call them rich and new,
When the poor sheep and silk-worm wore
That very clothing long before.

The tulip and the butterfly
Appear in gayer coats than I;
Let me be dressed fine as I will,
Flies, worms, and flowers exceed me still.

The only time I loved that hymn was one Whit Sunday when my sister and I had to appear *without our new dresses!*

This superintendent, a farmer and fruit-grower, lived at Swanley, and for forty or fifty years, through all weathers, winter snow and summer heat, he walked three miles every Sunday morning to Eynsford chapel, in time to begin school at nine o'clock. We never knew him to be a minute out; he kept even better time than our clocks. When in doubt, we watched for him to pass our house, and, seeing him, knew it was time for us to run off as fast as we could. He spent the whole day at the chapel, but so did many others.

As soon as we were old enough, this used to be our Sunday programme: Seven o'clock prayer-meeting, nine o'clock Sunday school, half-past ten public worship, two o'clock Sunday school, three o'clock service, half-past five o'clock Sunday school prayer-meeting, six o'clock service. I remember once when we had attended all these and sat down to conclude with family worship, my brother, tired out, pleaded in pitiful voice, 'Father, read a *short* psalm.' We used to go home to breakfast, but took our dinner with us, and ate it in our own pew, which was just inside, and was comfortably curtained round; but tea we had with the rest in the vestry, and a very happy time the friends spent together. It was like the meeting of a great family, and they came from all the villages around, Kingsdown, Meopham, Ash, Sutton, Darent, Cray, Swanley, Shoreham, Sevenoaks, and perhaps other places. Farmers drove, and brought their families, and others walked. Nobody thought it a hardship to walk five or six miles to chapel. The devoutness, the piety, the Christian friendship and love, all seemed very beautiful to me, and the gladness was like that of the tribes that went up to Jerusalem. The joyousness of these Sundays was wonderful. The chapel was the centre of intense love and loyalty. I remember with what a burst of pure delight the opening hymn used to be sung:

> How did my heart rejoice to hear
> My friends devoutly say,
> In Zion let us all appear
> And keep the holy day.

That little plain chapel, with its whitewashed walls, its table pew, and unadorned gallery, was a veritable temple to the loving hearts of its worshippers. The church at Eynsford was a mother-church. Not only was its pastor, the Reverend John Rogers, a man of considerable intellectual power and great personal influence, but there were other striking preachers, who often took the afternoon service when the minister was otherwise engaged. Those were hard days for Dissent, and I think our people were pretty abundantly persecuted, but it is certain that they rejoiced in that tribulation. I remember hearing that my Grandmother Hearn was baptised in the river, and on her way home was followed by a mob of rough village folk, who seriously injured her by throwing stones and brickbats at her. Still later, when the baptistery was in the chapel, I was told how a wife was baptised whose husband sat in a pew a little way off with a loaded gun, with which he had declared he would shoot her when she came up out of the water. It was spoken of as one of the glorious triumphs of grace that at that service he was changed from a rebel into a repentant seeker of salvation.

Most of the people living at a distance returned to their homes at the close of the afternoon service, but not to be idle, so far as religious duties were concerned. In those days the family was all-important, and the obligations of children and parents received stern and unfailing attention. The children were questioned on Sunday evenings, not only on their lessons in school, but the sermons which they had heard, and every one was expected to repeat the text. Family prayer was as little likely to be omitted as breakfast or supper, and the sins of the children were visited with unflinching discipline. Parental authority was no dream in those days, but the greatest reality which sons and daughters knew. The father was the master and judge of the household, and straight and strong were the words he addressed to the company of servants and children gathered in the kitchen or the dining-room. 'Spare the rod and spoil the child' was a frequently quoted axiom, and the quoter almost always believed that it was from the Bible, and was originally spoken by Solomon.

We got on better than most, because our mother was our minister, and the lessons we had on Sunday evenings were those of love; but our home was conducted on strictly religious principles. Father always prayed for us individually. One special plea for me I remember because it was almost invariably uttered, 'Bless dear Polly, and grant that she may find favour with Thee, and with the people with whom she may come in contact.' I knew this was asked because I was so much more plain-looking and uninteresting than my brothers and sisters, and that my future prospect was a gloomy one, but I hoped it might prove truly an answered prayer. I record most thankfully that the one great blessing given to me all my life has been the grace and favour of the people among whom I have lived and worked.

Chapter Three

HOP-GARDEN MEMORIES

The following sketch, written for *The Christian World*, reveals a little bit of our family life:–

When we were children, one of the happiest days of the year was that on which we went 'a-hopping.' We lived on the direct road from London to Maidstone, and before our village was reached hop-gardens began to be seen, while a little below us the best hops were grown, and the largest acreage was given to their cultivation. That was before the time of cheap trips by rail, and the Londoners usually walked the distance, pushing the trucks, or wheeling the barrows which carried the few household goods, including the baby, that were needed for a prolonged stay in the country. A saucepan or kettle, one or two mugs, an old shawl and a couple of blankets were generally packed in the vehicle, which sometimes, instead of being pushed by hand, was drawn by an old horse or donkey. The passage of the 'hoppers' through our village was watched with interest, and there was one Sunday especially which they spent at rest on the route, sleeping in stables, coach-houses, or even doorways, when we had more of them than we liked; but they often travelled in picturesque processions, and made up very merry parties.

Our sympathies, however, were not with the strangers from London, but the village folk, who resented their intrusion as likely to keep down the wages and make the hop-gardens uncomfortable with dirt and bad language. The hop-picking season was of great consequence to the villagers. Money then earned was delightful, because it was extra, and provided many comforts which could not otherwise be secured. The year's rent was almost always paid out of 'hopping-money,' which also served to buy the coals for winter, and it was a settled and understood thing that each member of the family should have a new pair of boots or shoes at the end of the hop-picking work; also that if new jackets for the boys and new dresses for the girls were needed the only way to pay for them was to earn money at the 'bin.' So, of course, when we had our day in the hop-garden, we at once made our way to some old neighbour or hard-working widow, and volunteered our services.

From the time when we began to be aroused, between three and four o'clock in the morning, by the cheery laughter of the hop-pickers setting out to work, until our day came, we thought and talked of little else. And when, at last, dressed in lilac sun-bonnets and coloured pinafores, and carrying with us our dinner of bread-and-butter and apples to eat, and bottles of milk to drink, we started for the hop-grounds, there were no happier little people than we in all the world, especially if our gentle mother went with us, as she usually did, not only to take care of us but to enjoy the fun too.

What a cool, lovely walk it was across the white fields from which the corn had been carried, along the shady Kentish lanes, and over the green meadows! And there is not anything more beautiful than the English hop-gardens. Compared with them, all the vineyards of Europe – excepting, perhaps, those of Italy – are most uninteresting and disappointing. The vines of the Rhine and of Switzerland are only like kitchen gardens of French beans beside our graceful hops. It was a great pleasure to walk along scented avenues of them, with the tall bines interlacing overhead, and with the great three-lobed leaves, and pretty, soft, cone-like catkins making a graceful shade from the sun. Planted three together in a triangle, they had climbed up the twelve-feet-high poles, and were hanging in beautiful gold-green clusters at the top. But we had something more to do than admire the festoons and walk along the trellised way; and so we took side-cuts and followed the sounds of voices until we reached the cleared spaces in which the 'bins' were placed. Does everybody know what a hop-bin is? It is like a large sack, open length-wise at the side, and fastened to a wooden frame. The pickers stand by the side of the bin and drop the hops in. The hop plants are brought and laid over the frame by the 'pole-pullers,' whose duty it is to cut the bine and pull up the poles and bear them to the workers, who are ready to strip off the pretty clusters with great speed.

We always received a welcome, and were soon at work; those who were tall enough stood at the bin, and the others sat on heaps of poles and dropped the hops into baskets or bags, or open, turned-up umbrellas. We worked as fast as we could, each trying to fill his or her receptacle, and putting as few leaves as possible into the basket. The pungent aromatic scent of the hops and the pleasant work in the fresh air acted like a tonic, and talk and laughter and sweet song were heard in all parts of the ground. We did not sing Sankey's hymns, for they had not yet been written, but such old favourites as 'Grace! 'tis a charming sound,' and 'Guide me, O Thou great Jehovah,' would be raised, and groups of chapel-goers would sing them, the children's voices being the sweetest and heartiest of them all. I can never forget the triumph which once, after missionary meetings had been held in our villages, rang out in the hymn, 'O'er the gloomy hills of darkness, look, my soul, be still and gaze.'

But 'hopping' is very appetising work, and it was with wonderful relish that, at twelve o'clock, we forgot the blackness of our hands and the bitter taste on our lips, and ate our thick bread-and-butter. We made our way after dinner to the hedges and the woods, for hopping and nutting and blackberrying all come together, and the time is a right royal one. Some of us went rather far, and tarried a good while, but we always got back for tea, when the kettle was boiled over the wood fire, and the picnic was one never to be forgotten.

After tea there was more work, for the measurers would soon come round to put the hops into the bushel-baskets, and then empty them into the big hop-pockets. Those of us who had been idle, or had played truant, were always sorry then, for if the bushels told up well our friends were glad and grateful, because they were paid a shilling for each six or seven bushels that had been picked.

The time was the merriest then, for it was almost certain that one of the little ones would be caught up and tossed into the bin, and covered over with the soft hops, and there were such shriekings of laughter, and scamperings away, that the fun became quite riotous. Our father had probably arrived by that time, and we all went home together, then a happy family of six – father, mother, three girls and one boy – and I could weep because there is only one of us left to-day to tell the story.

Chapter Four

LOSS

It was perhaps when I was about ten that we had measles. Our mother, the gentle nurse of us all, unfortunately caught the infection, and was never strong afterwards. When we had sufficiently recovered to be out in the garden again, I suppose the stage of convalescence found us very weak, and in order to encourage us to stay in the open air, and put forth our little strength, mother bought us all skipping-ropes. We did not know how to use them, so she showed us on a never-to-be-forgotten evening. We stood around, merrily laughing at the sight of our mother skipping like a girl, while we counted the times she kept up. Suddenly she dropped the rope and leaned against the wall, holding her handkerchief to her lips, and I noticed that it was stained with blood.

That was the beginning of the end. The doctor was a frequent visitor at our house for a long time after. Mother was advised to try a specialist, and my first visit to London was on that occasion. We travelled on the coach, for there was no railway. The coach was an interesting institution in our village; it went every day from Maidstone to London and back, and called at Farningham at an inn opposite our house to change horses. My mother appeared very sad and tired as we came home. I did not know then that she had received her death sentence. She kept about as long as she could, and then took to her bed, on which she lay for many months.

Dear, tired mother! she had worked very hard for us all, and it must have been a sore trial to be inactive and suffering in bed while we needed her so much downstairs. A few days ago, while turning over some old papers, I discovered her will. It is dated Farningham, June 30, 1846, and begins thus: 'I, Rebecca Hearn, feeling myself growing weaker, and being convinced that I shall never revive, desire in the event of my death that the few following things may be given and received as tokens of affectionate remembrance.' Then followed the disposal of her few possessions amongst us all, including her mother and four sisters. The pathetic document thus concludes: 'I desire to commend my dear husband and children to the guidance and care of our never-failing Friend. I hope my dear children will be kind and affectionate to each other, dutiful and obedient to their dear father and those who may have the care of them, and as they grow up be industrious and careful, and above all, oh, that they may be led early to seek the Lord Who has said, 'I love them that love Me, and those that seek Me early shall find Me.' I now desire to commit myself into His gracious hands, begging Him to prepare me for whatever He has prepared for me, and to –

> Assure my conscience of her part
>   In the Redeemer's blood,
> And bear Thy witness with my heart
>   That I am born of God.

> When I to death draw near
>   Then Jesus, look to me;
> Dispel my every fear,
>   And bid me come to Thee.

> And, oh, may I like Stephen prove,
> The sweet supports of Jesus' love.

REBECCA HEARN

My father told me some years afterward that these pleading sentences were quite characteristic of my mother. She was a very humble-minded Christian, who felt her own unworthiness too greatly to have much triumph of faith and assurance of acceptance. She was a lowly follower of the Lord Jesus Christ, and she had much of His spirit in her character and life; she was a tender, loving, reverent, self-forgetful Christian; a wise, devoted, prayerful, watchful mother; a beautiful woman in appearance, graceful in all her actions, whose life was a revelation of consecrated and absolute love.

I used to sit and sew in her bedroom, and read to her from a book called *The Dying Christian*, and oftener talk to her, and listen to what she said. She was never a great talker, but I remember that she had a whimsical way of putting even grave and serious things, and that she always seemed to me cheerful and bright whenever I was allowed to be with her. I was a long time being made to believe that she must really die, and I remember my impassioned prayers to God to spare her. She was so much more to us than our father that again and again I sobbed out this beseeching petition, 'O Lord, if you must have one, please take our father to heaven, and leave us our dear mother.' Indeed, my life at that time was one long prayer: 'Spare my mother. Do not be so cruel to us little children as to take our mother away.' At last, in my despair, I cried, 'O Lord, let us all die when mother dies, if she must.'

It was on Christmas Day that she died, the anniversary of her marriage. That Christmas Eve burnt itself into my soul. To this day I do not know how to bear the sounds of Christmas bells and carol-singers. I stood alone in a dark room, my brother and sisters having been sent to bed, pressing my hot, tear-stained face against the window-pane, and peering out into the darkness at the singers. While they sang 'Hark, the herald angels sing,' I felt as if all the light of my life went out, and that the Babe of Bethlehem could never be anything more to me again; and when the bells rang out their merry peal I hated them, and shrank from their sounds as if they were blows.

I lay awake all night. Toward morning, I heard my aunt advise my father to lie down for a little time, and then, in what seemed an hour later, I heard her open his door, and whisper, 'Joseph come; she is going.' I wanted to run in, but my impression is that I fainted, for I was found on the floor when it began to get light. Never, surely, did sadder Christmas break than that which looked on our little house at Farningham, and its motherless children, myself the oldest, and therefore the saddest of them all.

I very well remember going to the funeral, four little black-robed figures. I walked with my father next to the coffin, behind us the other three, Rebecca, Hephzibah, and Tom, the last poor little fellow only just able to toddle. Then came my mother's father and mother, and after them a long procession of her brothers and sisters, for they were a large family. There was a great company of mourners, for most of the villagers of both Farningham and Eynsford attended. Somebody put into my trembling hands, after it was all over, this text, 'As one whom his mother comforteth, so will I comfort you, and ye shall be comforted' (Isaiah lxvi, 13).

Chapter Five

GIRLHOOD

My father often said that I never had a girlhood, but grew at once from a child into a woman.

Certainly the responsibilities of life pressed very heavily upon me from the time of my mother's death. At first the aunt whom we loved, Miss Mary Bowers, who nursed my mother through her last illness, lived with us, and we had a few months of subdued peace and happiness. She was a sweet woman, whom everybody loved, and she was very tender and good to us; but she herself only lived a little while, I think less than a year, after her sister.

The death of our aunt made a sad difference to our home, and we children never had womanly care afterwards. A young cousin lived with us for some months, but she was scarcely any older than I. When I think of that time, the formative period of a girl's life, I am filled with thankfulness to the kind Providence who watched over me and my sisters, so young, and so unprotected. My father, though I did not know it, had at the time pressing financial difficulties which worried him, and made things harder for us all. I used to wish he would give us a step-mother, for I felt then, and feel still, that though it may be hard to have an unsympathetic step-mother, it is yet harder for motherless children to be without a woman to look after them. Of course I had to leave school and do the 'housekeeping' and the work of the house, and I am sure that it was done very badly. But I was only twelve years and a few months old, and the others were younger. We were left very much to ourselves, and I still think it was a bad time for a girl to pass through.

Reading was my chief consolation, and I had not much time for that. My father gave us two monthly magazines published by the Sunday School Union, *The Teacher's Offering*, and *The Child's Companion*. In one of these was a series of descriptive articles on men who had been poor boys, and risen to be rich and great. Every month I hoped to find the story of some poor ignorant *girl*, who, beginning life as handicapped as I, had yet been able by her own efforts and the blessing of God upon them to live a life of usefulness, if not of greatness. But I believe there was not a woman in the whole series. I was very bitter and naughty at that time. I did not pray, and was not anxious to be good.

But there were a few people who loved me, especially a Sunday school teacher; and it was love that saved me. One Sunday morning, as I sat with our class in the gallery, my head was throbbing and my heart was burning with indignation and anger. My teacher beckoned me to sit next to her, and when the sermon began she gently took my hand in hers. My first impulse was to draw it back, for I was in antagonism with the whole world, but there was a look of infinite compassion in her eyes that drew me to her. A very short sermon it seemed that day, and as it proceeded all bitterness died out of my heart. At first compunction, then penitence, then resolve, then peace, took possession of me, and I was quite another child when the service came to an end, for my heart was full of love and joy.

This teacher was my namesake, though not related to me. She was Miss Eliza Hearn, of Eynsford, and at this time mistress of the British school. I recall her as a little winsome lady, young and pale, and very gentle. She was always good to me, and I longed to go to day-school again that I might be with her. By fits and starts I went, but very irregularly, and my sisters did not fare much better than I. After a year or two we had everything to do, washing, mending, scrubbing, cooking. Poor father, his must have been the hardest lot of all!

Miss Hearn did a good deal for me and for the rest of the girls in many ways. Sixty years ago the elementary education of the British schools was carried on by very different methods from those of the Council schools of the present day. The great book of the school was the Bible. The teachers were not obliged to pass government examinations, but they were required to be members of some Christian Church, and to love, revere, and teach the Book of books. The first hour of every morning was devoted to religious instruction. We sang a hymn, and our teacher prayed with us, after which we repeated a prayer ourselves. Then we had a long Bible-lesson, the most interesting and important of the whole day. Miss Hearn gave the lesson herself, and taught it very thoroughly. She must have been an excellent teacher, her lessons were vivid and impressive, and they remained with us. Even now I can remember some of them. Not content with the morning scripture-lesson, the Friday afternoon of each week was given to religious instruction. This was really an evangelistic service for children, and our teacher would speak to us individually and very earnestly, using her influence to urge us to give ourselves to God. Somehow there was another look on her face and there were other tones in her voice when she talked to us about our Saviour. I am sure that her pleading words and Christian life had a great influence on the elder girls. But what would school managers say to such a teacher now?

The Hearn family group: Tom and Hephzibah standing, Mary Ann and their father Joseph Hearn seated.

One of my greatest regrets, even now, is that my attendance at the Eynsford British school was so perfunctory and intermittent. It was all the schooling that I had, and it can well be imagined that it has been exceedingly difficult to follow out the various pursuits of my life without any learning worth the name. I am so glad that compulsory education has been secured for the children of these happier days.

My father was the village postmaster. I helped him to sort the letters, and whenever there was an address in a particularly good handwriting, I copied it and tried to imitate it. I remember being told later that there was no style of my own in my handwriting – it was little wonder!

My ignorance was a constant burden to me, and I tried many devices to lessen it. Fond of reading as I was, I did not really enjoy the study of lesson-books, but I strove to make myself learn from them. Through one summer I rose at five o'clock every morning and went out with a book in my hand, but out-of-doors in the dewy meadows, or in the woods, vocal with the song of birds, I really could not study any printed book, and getting up early made me too tired. Our days were in any case long enough. My father was an early riser, and, during the summer months especially, he liked to have us all up. 'Come, my dears,' he used to say as soon as the clock struck six, 'the beautiful sun is shining upon you, and it is between six and seven!' By this time circumstances were more satisfactory with us.

My father was peculiarly good in many ways. In our worst days there were certain things that we never had to do. He did not believe that cleaning shoes was a girl's work, and on cold winter mornings we never came downstairs without finding a cheery fire burning in the grate ready for us, and a look of cosy comfort in our living-room. Then, too, excepting in those sad times when we, or others, had vexed him, he was always bright and kind, and full of fun and jokes; and if we ventured to invite our friends to tea he could always be trusted to be good to them, and to enter into our little social enjoyments as heartily as we did ourselves. We used not to bother him beforehand with any thought of expense or trouble! We had high times making cakes and tarts, but always when he was out of the way. Yet I never remember an angry word, either at the time or afterward. He took the good things and enjoyed them with the rest of us, and paid the bills in due course. But we knew better than to let these festivities occur too frequently.

In my desperate pursuit after knowledge I tried hard to burn the midnight tallow (we had no oil in those days), and many a 'long eight' have I wasted in the attempt. We were sent to bed before ten, but I was always sleepy, and resorted to one very immoral device to keep myself awake. When making tea for the family in the afternoon, after having infused the leaves, and before filling the pot, I used to pour off a cup of this strong decoction, and surreptitiously take it into my bedroom. I am afraid my father never knew this. I must have had a good digestion, or it would certainly have been ruined by the quantities of cold, strong tea I imbibed late at night. Of course I knew my father would not approve of my studying at midnight, and I was wretched in doing it. Once my heart sank within me as I listened to a conversation between him and a man who had come into the post-office.

'Is there any one ill at your house, Mr Hearn?'

'No, thank you; I am happy to say we are all pretty well.'

'Oh, I am glad to hear it. I was afraid somebody was ill. I had to be out last night looking after a horse, and I saw a light burning in one of your bedroom windows, between twelve and one o'clock.'

'Ah,' said my father, 'not for long, I suppose?'

'Yes; it was burning when I first went by, and still burning when I came back.'

I wished I could hide somewhere, but knew I must face the matter out. My father looked very judicial. 'Now, Polly, I suppose you heard what Mr Sharp said.'

'Yes father; there was a light in our room. I was trying to study. I am ashamed of myself for being ignorant, and you know you cannot spare me to go to school.'

'But what were you doing?'

'I was learning some geography.'

'Fetch your books down and show them to me.'

I brought down some cheap copy-books, with badly written pages, full of descriptions of the places that I dreamed about, and never hoped to see. My father said that he did not think such knowledge would ever be of much use to me. He said it was not honourable of me to say 'Good night' to him at the door and pretend I was going to bed, and then wait up to read. It was setting the others a bad example, and I was never to do it again. For a long time I did not, and then yielded to temptation once more. But the days made me so sleepy that even the strong tea failed to keep me awake, and frequently I have been so tired that I have lain down intending to get a short nap, and have only waked at six the next morning, cold and cramped, with all my clothes on, and the candle burnt down in the socket.

One night I awoke in terror, for the room was full of smoke. The candle was broken in the middle, and had bent over, and set the fringe on the dressing-table alight. The flames spread quickly, and already the hangings of the bed were on fire. I saw that it was hopeless for me to cope with it. On the impulse of the moment I opened the window, and in a second the whole room seemed to be in flames. In an agony of fear I called my father instantly. He was always a good friend in trouble, and he succeeded in extinguishing the fire. I was more dead than alive when I began to undress, and thankful to creep into bed. I remember he kissed me, and all he said was, 'I should think that now you have had enough of this, and that in the future you will see it is wisest to obey your father.'

I felt it only too deeply.

Perhaps it was really as a result of this that my father began to consult with me as to the possibility of my going to school again. He said that he could not afford to keep me without work, but since I was so very anxious to learn, and my sisters were growing older, he thought I might go to school for part of the days. He asked me if I would like to learn to do the shoe-binding. He told me that he paid away a good deal of money every week for having this done, and thought I could do it, if I would like to try. I said I would like it very much. He promised to show me how it was done, and told me that he would pay me, but added that I must pay him back something for my board and lodging, and have anything that was over for myself. I soon became rather an expert binder, and was particularly praised for my buttonholes; but I had hard work with one thing and another, and I did not begin to be rich. Indeed, I was generally in my father's debt, but I went to school again, always taking my work with me to do in the dinner hour, and glad at heart to be with my beloved Miss Hearn once more, and to grow a little less ignorant every week.

About this time, when I was perhaps fourteen, the minister at the Baptist chapel at Eynsford was the Reverend William Reynolds, who was an astronomer, and had a very fine telescope. He lived in the house in which Mr Rogers had died – the next but one to ours – and was very neighbourly, appearing to take a most kindly interest in me. I spent many an evening in his study, looking through the telescope, and learning many wonderful things about the sun, moon, and stars, all of which I am sorry to say I have quite forgotten now. I think his difficulty as a teacher of astronomy was that he could not comprehend the extreme ignorance of his pupil, and make allowance for a young mind that was then, and indeed was always, utterly unscientific. But he was very good to me in many ways, lending me books, and talking to me on all sorts of subjects.

One thing he did which I have ever thought much too bad.

My sister Rebecca was an exceedingly pretty girl, with the loveliest eyes and the longest lashes I have ever seen. She was very trim and dainty in her dress, and attractive in her manners. It was only natural that she cared a little for the simple pleasures (they were not many) that were possible in our village. The great worldly day of the year was Farningham Fair day, October 15th. We were never allowed to go to the fair. Our part was to watch the people pass by, all dressed in their best attire, and occasionally to hear reports of the shows and dances, and all the gay things that were done there. Rebecca had a great desire to go.

It happened that she had a very pretty new dress and hat, and we knew that she would have looked as sweet as the best. A neighbour who was going to take her own little girls invited Rebecca to join them, so my sister told me about it and asked my advice. I advised her to go by all means. 'There can be nothing really wicked in going to a fair,' I said, 'and I do not know why we should not have good times like other girls.' We decided not to say anything about it to our father until afterwards, when we might perhaps confess. Of course, if we had asked permission, and he had said 'No,' it would have ended the matter; but we decided that she should run the risk, so we said she had been asked out to tea to a neighbour's, as she had. She went, spent a couple of hours in the field, and came home quite early, her sweet face all aglow with pleasure. We felt that we had done a very bold thing, but we were quite unprepared for what followed.

Mr Reynolds had himself given up that afternoon to the fair; that is, he had adjusted his telescope so as to get the field in full view, and he had picked out all the people whom he knew, especially my sister, whom he watched a long time. He was beforehand with us in regard to our confession, for he told my father, and we were summoned before them. The minister described what he had seen, and 'more in sorrow than in anger' the two men talked to us about our great sin. I had the worst of it, as being the eldest of the family who ought to have a better influence over my sister. The only excuse I could offer was that I wanted her to go and enjoy herself, and I said I wished to know all about the fair myself. We two poor little offenders stood before our judges, wondering what punishment would be meted out; but our worst fears fell short of the reality. We were not beaten, nor shut up; what did occur was that Mr Reynolds spoke of the thing on Sunday, in his sermon. He mentioned no names, but our faces burned with shame, and all the congregation knew that 'Rebecca Hearn had been to the fair.' I think to-day that it was very mean of the minister, and I believe that our father had much more sympathy with us than with him in regard to the affair.

After my teacher, Miss Hearn, left the neighbourhood, I was put into the senior class at Sunday school. The teacher was Miss Isabella Rogers, my father's cousin, afterwards Mrs Creasey, of whom I have already spoken as having taught me to write. It was while I was in her class, and when I was between fourteen and fifteen years of age, that I became possessed by a desire to join the Church. No one, I think, had before that time become a member at so early an age, and the minister, though exceedingly pleased with my wish, was a little in doubt. Was I able to give a reason for 'the hope that was in me'? I do not think that I was very well able. I knew so little, and it was not an easy thing to enter a Church that was both Calvinistic and Strict Baptist. Mr and Mrs Reynolds were kind to me, and my friend and teacher, Miss Rogers, treated me with a tender solicitude, the memory of which warms my heart to-day. After several interviews with the pastor, he told me that he would bring my name before the Church at the next meeting. Two deacons were appointed to see me, and when I heard the name of one, Mr Cooper, a farmer who lived at Ash, I felt sure that the Church would not accept me, because only a few Sundays before, during the morning service, he had come out of his seat and walked across the gallery on purpose to rebuke me for laughing. However, he seemed to have forgotten the circumstance, and was surprisingly kind.

The difficulty was that I could not remember when I was converted or if I ever had been. There was no special time. I had not been heart-broken for my sins, nor had I passed through any terrible phase of repentance. I had never wept on my knees, nor spent whole nights in prayer, as some of my friends and companions had done. All I knew was that I loved and trusted the Saviour, and believed that He was able to save and keep me, and that I wanted, above all else, to serve and please Him. A few things I remembered that had impressed me – my mother's life and death, my father's prayers, and the love of two or three Christian women. My impulse and desire were toward religion. I loved the Bible, and the house of God was dear to me. I have often risen an hour earlier in the morning and hurried through a hard day's work that I might go to the prayer-meeting in the evening. Several persons had exercised a most beneficent influence on me. There was one, Mary Thorpe, who worked in the paper-mill, but who was a refined Christian gentlewoman, and who was for some time my Sunday school teacher. She held the class in a square pew of the chapel. It consisted of five or six girls, and I think that every one of us was loved and prayed into trying to be good by her. But I could name no definite experience or time that marked my passing from carelessness to earnestness.

I often wonder what I said that satisfied the deacons, for I suppose they were satisfied, as I was asked to come before the Church at the next meeting. This was a trying ordeal. I sat on a form in the middle of the vestry. The minister and deacons sat in a square place, with their backs to the window, and the other members of the Church were in various seats around. The minister was very gentle, but he put a good many close questions to me. 'Why do you think that you are saved?' 'Because I love the Lord Jesus Christ.' 'What about good works?' 'I have none. It is all of grace.' This I knew was the answer he wanted. Certain questions respecting election, predestination, and justification were put to me, but beyond saying that they were scriptural doctrines I do not know what I replied. I wish I did, for my answers must have been very curious. But one thing I knew, and know still, that these Calvinist and Strict Baptists lived, for the most part, very beautiful lives, that they were obviously set apart from the rest of the people, that their Christian joyousness was wonderful, and that I longed to be as they were. Young people who join our Churches to-day find their entrance into the fold less barred than I did.

I must have been born a Baptist. Not a doubt assailed me as to the proper persons to receive baptism, nor the mode in which it was to be given. 'The disciples first believed, then were baptised, then were added to the Church.' Mr Reynolds put one question to me, which I answered glibly enough. 'Would you think it unscriptural to take the Lord's Supper with unbaptised believers?' I thought for a moment, 'Who were unbaptised believers?' At that time our chapel was the only Nonconformist place of worship for many miles around. Later a Wesleyan cause was started at Farningham, but then only the Church of England and the Baptists occupied the ground. I concluded that the question must refer to the Church people, and I am afraid that I had no doubt that they were the believers who were wrong. Certainly I never went to church, if that was what Mr Reynolds meant, and I expressed the opinion that it *was* unscriptural to take the Communion with others than Strict Baptists! I retained that opinion for nearly a whole year afterward, but happily not longer, and always I have loved the Church service.

The picture of myself as I sat there, a child among the elders, often recurs to me. I was small for my age. I remember that I wore a lilac print dress, and it was, I think, the first dress I had worn with long sleeves. I was very much in earnest. I longed with a great longing that this little company would accept me as a member, and receive me into their midst, and allow me to be baptised, and take the Lord's Supper with them. I felt that I was very unworthy, young, and poor, and of no account, but my one plea and qualification was that I was full of love to Jesus and His people. It was because with all my youthful fervour I wanted to follow my Lord and obey His commands, that I asked to be baptised. I was very nervous and frightened, but presently the minister asked me to retire for a few minutes, while they consulted about me. I went out into the chapel ground among the trees, for the moments of suspense that followed. I scarcely dared to hope that their decision would be favourable; but it was my father who called me back, and there was a happy look on his face as he kissed me.

'Marianne,' said Mr Reynolds, 'we are all very much interested in what you have told us, and the friends have decided to receive you into Church fellowship after baptism.'

It was almost more than I could bear, and I had to choke back my tears.

Then the minister talked to me. He said that Christ had kept His promise

'Those who seek Me early shall find Me,' and that His power would be able to keep me faithful to the end. He reminded me that I had only to live a day at a time, and grace sufficient had been promised. He told me that after drawing attention to myself by a public profession of my faith, my conduct and life would be very closely watched. 'We shall watch you narrowly, and prayerfully, to see whether you walk consistently, and adorn the doctrines which you have professed. The world, the enemies of Christ will watch you, and be quick to see if in anything you fall away. And Christ will watch you to see if you bring dishonour on His cause and name. Remember that you have no power in yourself to stand; your sufficiency must be of God, and to Him we commend you.' I felt that it was all very solemn; but as the meeting concluded the minister and the deacons besought for me the grace that I needed.

I was baptised on a lovely Sunday evening in June, Miss Rogers standing by me: and I took my first communion, with heavenly gladness in my soul, on the following Sunday.

Chapter Six

BEGINNINGS

Early in the year 1852 the oversight of the Baptist church, at Eynsford, was taken by the Reverend Jonathan Whittemore. Mr Whittemore was born at Sandy, in Bedfordshire, in the year 1802. At a very early age he resolved to be a minister, and found his recreation in preparing sketches of sermons. The real work of his life began when he entered the publishing business of his relative, Mr Baynes, of Paternoster Row. Henceforward, publishing and preaching occupied all his powers.

Mr Whittemore's arrival at Eynsford introduced a new interest into the church life there. His ministerial abilities might have found a far larger sphere, but the lanes and fields and hop-gardens of this lovely part of Kent attracted him, and especially the fact that Eynsford is only twenty miles from London, where he spent the middle of most weeks. His talk about books and newspapers and publishing matters generally quickened in the minds of several young people a latent desire to write. I had already written rhymes for friends' birthdays, and other local happenings. When, through any accident, these fell into Mr Whittemore's hands, I always had a bad time. He would make me listen while he read them to me, laying strong emphasis on their faults and weaknesses, and with most aggravating scorn in his voice. I kept on, however, in spite of his adverse opinion, only being careful to pledge my friends to secrecy. A little girl, connected with our family, died, and I wrote some verses and sent them to the child's mother, a lady of fine intellectual ability. She wrote a short account of her daughter, and put my verses in it. Mr Whittemore read this account during his funeral sermon. There was no name attached to the verses, and he, believing them to have been written by the lady herself, said, before reading them, 'I do not know the author of these lines, but they are very beautiful.' I was quietly sitting in our pew at the back of the chapel, with my father, and I had a moment of keen joy, not unmixed with pride, for I knew that nothing would have induced him to speak thus had he known the words were mine.

But I owe everything to Mr Whittemore's criticisms of my first efforts, which made me more painstaking. It was soon after this that I was ambitious enough to send twelve verses to a magazine, called, I think, *The Gospel Magazine*. The title was 'Music in Heaven.' Of course, in those early days I knew all about that subject! The magazine appeared every month, and after the lapse of twelve my poem was printed, and occupied exactly a page.

In the same year that Mr Whittemore came to Eynsford, 1852, I went to Bristol. A friend, Miss Bamford, who had been the mistress of the British school at Eynsford, removed to the Western City, and I became her assistant in the Durdham Down school. This change was a very interesting and pleasant one to me. All my life had been spent in villages, and this delightful old city appealed to my imagination, while the larger life, which I enjoyed there, was a wonderful education. Its quays and bridges, its narrow streets and old houses, its cathedral and old churches, its ships and boats and rivers were a constant source of fascination to me. In imagination, I watched the ships go out over the great sea, and arrive at their destinations in foreign countries. I had never seen a ship before, or a great river, and the sea was at that time only a dream. Every walk, therefore, had some new wonder to reveal to me, of life and activity. A walk down the 'Steps' and through the streets was a holiday. It seemed to me that there was a great difference between the men of Kent and the Bristol men, and it was always a treat to talk with the West Country people. Indeed, I fell in love with them from the first, a love which has lasted for the rest of my life.

Everybody I met seemed to show me some kindness. Miss Bamford and I were invited to a teacher's picnic. It was held in the beautiful woods by the side of the picturesque Severn, and the lofty hills and rich scenery filled my heart with gladness. The teachers, too, were all most kind people. Miss Matilda Lewis was especially good to the plainly dressed, timid little stranger from Kent, and we there commenced a friendship which has remained unbroken for more than fifty years. She, too, was a Baptist, and sang in the choir of Counterslip church, and she advised me to attend the services there, which I did, listening when possible to the Grand Old Man, called 'Father Winter.'

Sometimes I attended the cathedral, and I well remember being present there at a Memorial Service on the day of the funeral of the Duke of Wellington. For the first time I heard the Dead March in Saul, which affected me greatly. The place, of course, was crowded, but being small and resolute, I managed to push my way up to the very front, and I have never forgotten that I sat among the white-robed singers in the choir, one of whom made room for me just inside one of the stalls, and allowed me to look over his book. I felt very proud, but then I was only seventeen! The way in which I got out of the crowd also remains in my memory. I suppose I felt faint and looked white, for a gentleman took me up and carried me through as the crowd made way for us, and I found myself out in the cool air in a very short time.

I enjoyed teaching in the Durdham Down school where I had charge of the highest class of girls. I knew very little, but was able to impart to them every scrap of information I possessed. I could not have passed an examination, but in those happy days it was not required of me, and I had spent a few weeks at the Home and Colonial College on my way down. The girls were good and teachable, and we were all interested together, for I learned the lessons they learned, and was like one of them. The time passed all too quickly, for it was full of life and interest.

When I had been at Bristol a year I had a very sad letter from my father, telling me that my sister Rebecca, next to me in age, was ill, and the doctor had pronounced it to be consumption. My sister was a lovely girl, and she looked like a strong and completely healthy one. It did not seem possible that she could be really seriously ill. But my father's letter was very grave, and he told me that I must come home as soon as I could be released from school. So I gave a month's notice, and at the end of the time, with a heavy heart, I said good-bye to Bristol, and as I then thought, to all my best prospects in life.

I was glad to be at home again, and went with many resolves to be a better housekeeper than before I left home. I was a year older, with a year's experience, and was able to bring to my domestic work an increase of knowledge and patience. I had a loving welcome home, especially from my dear sister. It was easy to see, since the memory of my mother's illness remained with me, that Rebecca was following her. The mischief began at a midnight meeting, which she had walked through snow to attend, and to pray the old year out and the new year in. She dated her conversion from this meeting, which was therefore the beginning of a new life, as well as the beginning of the end. 'Surely something can be done which will prolong her life,' I said to the doctor. 'Well, if you can take her away to the south of France,' the doctor replied, 'it is possible that she might live a few years instead of a few months.'

Of course that was utterly impossible, and so we had that very common experience of the poor. We watched our dear one get worse and weaker day by day, only putting off the end as far as we were able. But those months have always seemed to me a most sacred time. She was so bright and patient, and even happy. She had a very blessed realisation of the Presence of Christ with her all the time. She was greatly beloved, and our little home became often a sanctuary of prayer and praise. When she passed away to the heaven that was so real to her, it seemed to be wonderfully near to us also.

During my sister's illness, when sitting with her in the garden, or watching by her bed at night, my thoughts had frequently set themselves into verse, and after her death I occasionally sent copies to magazines, saying nothing to anybody about them, and usually signing them 'Echo.' It struck me as something to be grateful for then, and does so still, that I never had one returned to me. It was two or three years after my 'Music in Heaven' had appeared in the magazine that I sent a poem of ninety lines to *The Christian Cabinet*, a religious paper, which was then in circulation, and was afterwards incorporated with *The Christian World*. The title of the poem was 'Let us Pray,' and it was inserted in the next number. Then Mr Whittemore said that he must have a serious talk with me.

He began by asking me why I had not submitted the verses to him, since I knew of *The Baptist Messenger* which he edited. I replied that, because he had always ridiculed my efforts, I had not supposed that he would care to have anything I might write, and so had sent this poem to one who did not know me. He told me it was very cowardly to shrink from criticism, which was intended to do me nothing but good. I answered that I knew quite well that was true, but that I found his criticisms all the harder to bear because he was so sarcastic. If, however, he wished to have some contributions from me, I should be only too glad to hand them over. He told me of a new tune-book which he was bringing out, and invited me to try to write hymns for some of the new tunes, and presently he took me into confidence in regard to quite a number of magazines and journals which he was projecting. Eventually he talked to me of what was the greatest hope of his life – a weekly religious paper, with very high aims, in which some of the leading wealthy Nonconformists of the time would interest themselves, and in which he thought I might help him.

These years at home were very joyous ones. Happily I had another sister, Hephzibah, who loved and helped me. She was more sensible and domesticated than I. Indeed, she was remarkably gifted in all the sweet mysteries of household ways, for certainly she had no one to teach her, since she was only a child of six when our mother died. She cared for me with almost more than a sister's love, and gave me time to write and study. Our brother Tom was a merry boy, and we three contrived to get all the pleasure possible out of life at this juncture, with our father to help us.

Most of our social life centred in the chapel. On my return from Bristol, when I offered my services to the superintendent to take a class in the school, he told me that the girls of the Bible class, being without a teacher, had asked that I would take it. I was fairly nonplussed by this suggestion, and said that I could not do it, for I was no older than the other girls, and certainly knew no more than they. He said that I could study the lesson during the week, and he hoped I would try. The girls themselves came to see me, and declared that they would not leave until they had persuaded me. So I yielded, and promised to do my best. We had a good many very happy Sunday afternoons. We were a class without a teacher, but everybody contributed something, and whether or not we learnt much, we carried away from that corner pew many pleasant memories. I have still in my possession, and indeed not many days pass without my using it, a copy of Cruden's *Concordance* with which the girls presented me, and with my name written in it by Mr Henry Rogers, the superintendent of the Sunday school. It has been worth its weight in gold to me. The inscription bears date 17 December 1857.

What glorious times we had, attending every service for which the chapel was opened! Our Sunday walks to and fro were delightful. I always felt we were like the glad tribes going up to Jerusalem. There would be a long line of us, ten or a dozen young people of both sexes, marching along and singing as we went, so that the mile between the two villages seemed as nothing. We would sing 'All hail the power of Jesus' name,' to Miles Lane, or 'Sweet is the work, my God, my King,' to Montgomery, a capital tune to march to, though there was one better still which we always sang when the moon shone or the stars were unusually bright, 'The spacious firmament on high.' I never hear this sung now without wanting to keep time with my feet, as I did in those good old days. I often wonder whether the village chapels can be as much to those who worship in them to-day as they were to us.

I had some exceedingly kind friends and companions at this time, in better circumstances and better educated than I, whom it was a great joy to be with. I visited at their houses, they called for me to take walks with them, and they lent me books. But Mr Whittemore did most for me in this way. One day he brought me a copy of *Jane Eyre*. 'Here is a book, my girl,' he said, 'that is thrilling everybody. If you can write like this, you will do somthing.' Alas! I only wished I could, and have been wishing it ever since. I had no sleep that night, and it haunted me for many nights afterwards. I had been taught that it was wicked to read novels, and this one marked my departure from that old limitation. Mr Whittemore also gave me my first and only copy of Shakespeare, writing in it my name and the words, 'From her affectionate pastor.' A great deal of trouble he had in consequence. That a minister should give a young member of his church 'a volume of plays,' seemed to some of the old members an outrageous thing. One anxious lady begged me to let her burn it, as she was sure it was an offence in the sight of God, and several who heard of it advised me not to read it; but of course it brought me into a new world, and filled me with wonder and admiration. One thing surprised me very much; it was to find some expressions which I had quite thought were only to be found in the Bible! Naturally I place a very high value on that copy of Shakespeare.

So I was living and learning and loving, until my happy teens were left behind. I had a grand time on my twenty-first birthday. How it was managed I do not know, but we were a party of twenty-one to tea, in our little house, which could never have been intended to hold more than four. It was finely decorated for the occasion. Over the fireplace in the small parlour, a friend, Thomas Sharwood, to whom my sister was afterwards married, had put up, in letters made of leaves and berries, the motto, 'God bless dear Polly.' I had, indeed, a happy coming-of-age.

Appendix

POEMS*

Time to Hope

Open all the windows
  To the sun!
Winter's reign is over,
  Spring begun;
Darkness is departing,
  Skies are blue,
Distances are dawning
  The mists through;
After longest waiting
  Spring is won –
Open all the windows
  To the sun.

Signs of gloomy winter
  Still remain,
Last year's leaves lie sodden
  On the plain,
But the light stays longer
  In the street,
And about the garden
  Songs are sweet;
Give the flowers a welcome
  One by one –
Open all the windows
  To the sun.

---

* Together, Cut Corn, Blackberries, September, Serviceable and Through Tribulation are from *Harvest Gleanings and Gathered Fragments*; Time to Hope, A Summer Prayer, A Sea-Mist, What Makes Music?, Were They Mistakes? and Good-Speed! are from *Lyrics of the Soul*.

Take to heart the sunshine,
    Weary men,
After disappointments
    Hope again.
God will clothe the meadows
    In bright gold,
He will give you blessings
    New and old,
Triumph after failure
    Shall be won –
Open Faith's clear windows
    To the sun.

A Summer Prayer

Oh, send Thy summer to my soul,
    Lord of the changing times;
Make Thy grand music o'er me roll
    From sea and river chimes;
Give me my share of growth and good,
Like thriving corn and songful wood.

Thou givest more abundant life
    To wheat, and grass, and tree,
That rise and stretch in upward strife –
    Lord, give such strength to me.
Restore me with Thy Spirit's breath,
And let divine life conquer death.

O Sun of Righteousness, shine through
    The mists of sin and care,
Call fragrant blossoms, fresh and new
    To spaces rough and bare;
And, by the glory of Thy face,
Make my life show some signs of grace.

I lift my weary eyes to Thee,
    My Saviour and my King!
Extend Thy bounties unto me,
    And teach my lips to sing;
My times are under Thy control,
Lord, send Thy summer to my soul.

A Sea-Mist

It is the summer,
  Though the day is dim,
And there is music,
  Though we hear no hymn.
The banks are covered
  With a wealth of flowers,
Glad birds are singing
  In the far-off bowers,
The corn is waving
  On a thousand fields,
The purple moorland
  Still its heather yields,
No touch of beauty
  Has the Lord forgot –
It is the summer
  Though we see it not.

It is thy summer,
  Though the mists alone
Seem to encompass thee,
  And seas make moan;
The heavy clouds
  Shut out the fair blue sky,
But thou are not alone,
  For God is nigh;
The mountains of His strength
  Are round about,
His mercies do not cease
  For all thy doubt;
The fields of God are rich
  For thy receiving,
And all is well –
  Oh! be thou glad believing.

What Makes Music?

Last night we stood beneath the trees
And listened to their harmonies,
Wishing that life might easier be
With quiet times for you and me;
We told each other of our cares,
And echoed some unanswered prayers;
Yet hushed our talk sometimes to hear
The sweet leaf music soft and clear,
And felt that God and Love were near.

To-night the world is still and calm,
There is no sound of any psalm;
No leaf is ruffled, not a flower
Bends its sweet head in this hot hour.
There are no organ notes for us,
And you and I who listen thus
Find all things too inert to please,
Long vainly for the troubled breeze
To make the music in the trees.

Absolute calm is never bliss,
Better the lashing winds than this;
In sorrow greatest things are wrought,
In sorrow sweetest songs are taught!
Ah, friend! if e'er our lives should make
Music for others, for Love's sake,
Less in our quiet dreamful days
Shall we bless them and give God praise
Than when we pass through troubled ways.

Together

'Twas a summer of one of the yesterdays.
　Do you remember?
　From June to September
Life led us along its pleasant ways.
We talked and were silent, we sang and dreamed,
And had all the world to ourselves, it seemed;
There was sorrowless joy in the fresh, sweet air,
The fields and hedges were strangely fair,
And all things growing told us their hopes,
As we walked in the valleys or climbed the slopes;
The breeze kissed everything – kissed us, too –
And we learnt the birds' love-songs, I and you,
And oh, how we *lived* in that sunny weather,
　Together!

All things were glad in those radiant days,
　From June to September;
　Do you remember?
It was a summer too sweet to praise!
We stood together among the hay
When I dreamed there was something you wished to say;
We were afloat on the tranquil sea
When first I knew that you cared for me;
The sweet, wild roses were in the lane
When my heart awoke to a bliss, half pain;
And there never was such a day before
As that which we spent on the breezy moor,
When, sure of each other, we gathered the heather
　Together.

Long, long ago were those matchless days!
  Do you remember
  That June and September?
We have walked since then such different ways.
I think of it all to-day, but you,
Away up there beyond the blue –
I cannot be sure that you do not forget,
You have so much other to think of. Yet,
The best that we had on the earth was love,
And the source of it, home of it, is above;
So perhaps that summer was not the end,
And there may be a fairer one yet to spend
In a happier land, and in sunnier weather
  Together.

Cut Corn

Poor fields so plundered,
  Late wealthy with gold;
Poor smitten corn,
  Grown suddenly old!
Where is their beauty?
  Ruthlessly slain:
Low on the earth
  Lie the fair heads of grain.

Tall, bright and graceful
  The corn yesterday,
Now it is borne
  From its birthplace away.
Yet are no mourners,
  For nobody grieves;
Songs, and not tears,
  Are for harvests of sheaves.

Ah, it is better
  To die for men's aid
Than to smile and look lovely
  In forest or glade.
Not beauty, but usefulness,
  Reaches God's test;
The fields are for harvests,
  And cut corn is best.

Blackberries

Ah! the joy of the blackberry bushes
   Scrambling over the hedges and banks!
A psalm is sung through the autumn glory
   Thrilling with beauty, giving God thanks.
This is the fruit-harvest, free for the garnering,
   Ready and ripe for the children's hands;
Hurrah for the days that are bright and merry!
   Come out from the cities and over the lands.

The scarlet haws are alive on the hedges,
   Each acorn is filling its chaste, traced cup;
Red hips have taken the place of the roses,
   The forests are lifting their treasures up.
In the golden gleam of the wild crab apples,
   In the purple bloom of damson and sloe,
In the plentiful, generous, free blackberries,
   The harvest joy is for all to know.

What fun and frolic – do you remember? –
   We had with the berries when we were young;
When prophecies shone in the distant landscapes,
   And love was a dream and its songs unsung!
Now the distances lie behind us,
   Our feet have traversed much of the way,
But never was autumn more fair and peaceful,
   Nor blackberries lovelier than to-day.

Cheery lessons of faith and fealty
   Come to all through blackberry vines;
God seems the nearer, His love more gracious,
   When summer is gone and the year declines.
Who is afraid of the storm and tempest?
   This is the season for trust and thanks;
And hey! for the joy of the bonnie blackberries
   And the glory of God on hedges and banks!

September

Who dare call Queen September old?
   Her face is fair.
She does not stoop, she is not cold,
   But debonair.

She claims, 'tis true, a longer night
   For rest and sleep,
Nor will she, who respects her sight,
   Late vigils keep.

But her blue eyes are clear as youth
  When day returns,
And her cheek glows with love and truth
  When evening burns.

Rich, jovial, clothed in gayest dress,
  She spends the day,
And, with large-hearted lavishness,
  She gives away

Gold for the gleaner, for the thrush
  Harvests of food,
And for world-weary men the hush
  Of quiet wood.

She cares for children in her prime,
  And with them plays
The merry games of nutting time
  On royal days.

Yet wears her golden crown of state
  On brow serene,
And bears herself erect, elate,
  A charming Queen!

Through Tribulation

I have asked for thee plenteousness and peace,
Not the fierce strife of warfare, nor its cost;
I have dreamed of thee with the full increase
Of summer's glory, not a treasure lost,
Thy life all sunshine, music, joy, and rest –
Have I been wise? Are these things truly best?

Dear, look with me through distances that hide
The earth from heaven, the little from the great.
The radiant hosts upon the other side,
By fountains of cool waters, safe, elate,
Are they who out of tribulation came –
God's love for thee can bear to choose the same.

I trust thee to His love, and not my own;
My best, perhaps, would but impoverish thee.
If, clothed in white, thou standest by the throne,
And I may, humbly glad, thy rapture see,
Confessing my poor love not strong enough,
I will praise Him who made thy pathway rough.

Serviceable

I think the love that most your trust deserves
Is that which does not hesitate or doubt;
Which asks no burden, but lasts on and serves,
And which no years nor trials can wear out;
Which fails not, tires not on the roughest way,
And has a new birth every new-born day.

Dear, use me as you use all common things
Of which you know there is enough to spare,
Plenty for mornings and for evenings,
For summer psalms and winter's wear-and-tear.
Love such as mine takes up its song again
Alike in smiles of peace and sobs of pain.

Were They Mistakes?

I took a turning wrong
    At the parting of the ways,
But a lark poured down its song,
    And a thrush sang out its lays;
And all the way through meadows sweet
The flowers and grasses met my feet.

I did not see that chance
    Which might have led to wealth;
Love conquered circumstance,
    And a new life sprang to health;
But the dear sun kissed me from the sky,
Although I let that chance go by.

The friends I loved the best
    Were not the famed and great;
Would I have found more rest
    In things of high estate?
But there are winsome songs of praise
For loving hearts in lowly ways.

A choice was mine to make –
    God does not force our will;
But I think for love's own sake
    That was a good choice still;
And I can count, at set of sun,
For some things lost much treasure won.

Are they mistakes that lead
    Either to left or right?
God gives us at our need
    Surely the gleam of light.
The choice is ours – but He keeps yet
The ways wherein our feet are set.

Yes, it is now too late
    To climb the heights you show;
I am with those who wait
    And watch the evening glow;
But God's forgiveness keeps me calm,
And my heart sings a thankful psalm.

Good-Speed!

I watch you start: I wave my hand,
   Young traveller in the unknown way.
Before you stretch wide miles of sand
   Which you will tread ere close of day;
Fear not those spaces you must roam,
I know them – I am nearly home.

The sun may beat upon your head,
   But in the sultry afternoon
You find green resting-places spread
   Where you may lie, and strengthened soon
Resume the journey. Pilgrims know
Delightful rests – I found them so.

There may be stony hills to climb,
   So steep they tax your utmost strength,
But from the summit scenes sublime
   Reward the brightening eyes at length,
And, ah! the colours and the lights
On mountains! You will love the heights.

Some gloomy passes in thick shade
   May lie before, and hush your song;
Pass on, and do not be afraid,
   If they are dark they are not long;
I tell you this your heart to cheer,
There is not anything to fear.

You do not journey on alone,
   A friend goes with you all the way,
A Guide to whom each step is known,
   To whom the night is as the day,
A Helper able, kind and true –
I proved Him thus, and so will you.

His patience is most wonderful,
   You do not always think of Him,
But in some new Place Beautiful
   You lift your eyes with musings dim,
And He smiles back to you the same,
Love is not swift to chide and blame.

The Shepherd knows where pastures are,
   And where the cool sweet waters flow,
And let the light be sun or star
   You will be glad to have it so.
Dear Pilgrim, He goes on with you,
Whom I know well. Adieu! Adieu!

A Brief Chronology and Bibliography

1834　Mary Ann Hearn born in Farningham, Kent, 17th December
1846　Death of her mother, Rebecca Hearn
1852　To Bristol
1853　Death of her sister, Rebecca
1857　First issue of *The Christian World*
　　　To Gravesend
1858　*Echoes from Darenth Vale: Tales and Truths in Prose and Verse* (under name Marianne Hearn*)
1859　To Northampton
1860　*Lays and Lyrics of the Blessed Life* (poems)
　　　First issue of *The Sunday School Times & Home Educator*
1861　*Life Sketches and Echoes from the Valley* (1st series)
1863　*Morning and Evening Hymns for a Week*
1866　*Gilbert and other Poems*
1867　Becomes salaried member of staff on *The Christian World*
　　　Listening for the Bells
1868　*Chats by the Sea*
　　　Life Sketches and Echoes from the Valley (2nd series)
1869　*Girlhood*
　　　Home Life
　　　Little Tales for Little Readers
1870　*Under the Shadow*
　　　Boyhood
1871　*The Cathedral's Shadow*
　　　The Sunday Schools of the Future
　　　Life Sketches and Echoes from the Valley (3rd series)
1872　*Out of the Depths*
1873　*Leaves from Elim* (poems)
　　　The Clarence Family, or *Brothers and Sisters*
1874　*Dell's New Year*
　　　Sunday Afternoons with Jesus

* Except where otherwise shown, all works appeared under the name Marianne Farningham.

1875   *Grace Darling, the Heroine of the Farne Islands* (under name Eva
Hope)
1876   *The Summer and Autumn of Life*
What of the Night?
1877   *Will you take it?*
1878   *Songs of Sunshine* (poems)
The Children's Holidays
1880   *The Story of the Years*
1884   Introduction to The Canterbury Poets edition of Longfellow's poems
(under name Eva Hope)
1885   Becomes editor of *The Sunday School Times*
Introduction to The Canterbury Poets editions of the poems of
William Cowper and of John Greenleaf Whittier (under name Eva
Hope)
1886   *Homely Talks about Homely Things*
1887   *Souvenir of the Queen's Jubilee* (verse)
1888   Death of her brother, Tom
1889   Death of her father, Joseph Hearn
1892   *Nineteen Hundred? A Forecast and a Story*
1893   Death of her sister, Hephzibah
A Story of Fifty Years
New World Heroes (under name Eva Hope)
1897   *In Evening Lights*
1898   *A Window in Paris*
1903   *Harvest Gleanings and Gathered Fragments* (poems)
1904   *Women and their Saviour*
1906   *Women and their Work*
1907   *A Working Woman's Life* (autobiography)
1908   *Lyrics of the Soul* (poems)
1909   Death of Mary Ann Hearn at Barmouth, 16th March
Songs of Joy and Faith (poems, posthumous collection)
W. Glandwr-Morgan, *Marianne Farningham in her Welsh Home* (short
memoir)

Index